Map of S...
William ...
1747. This ...
measures put in place during the
Jacobite rebellion of 1745-6.

S E A

IFF

THE HOLMES

This Cliff was made Practicable

Charnel Garth

Paradise Close

Paradise House

Paradise Garden

High West Gate

Castle Gate

West Gate

Tutthill Street

Bambil Gate

HARBOUR

Castle Pier

Pier

ROCKS

A. Scale of Chains
1 2 3 4 5 6 7 8 9 10

IN Memory of the Loyalty of the Inhabitants of the Antient Corporation of SCARBOROUGH During the time of the Rebellion This Plate describing the Works they Voluntarily raised against His MAJESTY'S Enemys Is Most Humbly Inscribed To His GRACE John, DUKE of Montagu Master of the Ordnance &c. &c. &c. By His GRACE'S Most Obedient, Most Humble and Most Devoted Serv. William Vincent

Nath. Hill Sculp.

CASTLE GARTH

S E A

THE
CAPTAINS NAME S
That had their Guns Moun
in the New raised Batter
— Gu

Mr. Bayliff Dickinson
Mr. Jonas Rickinson
Mr. Ford Newton
Mr. Frans. Goland
Mr. Robt. Grainge
Mr. Tho. Maling
Mr. Robt. Garbut
Mr. Willm. Garbut
Mr. James Hotlend
Mr. Frans. Gott
Mr. John Glover
Mr. Step. Gisbrough
Mr. John Hebden
Mr. Chris. Wilson
Mr. Willm. Wilson
Mr. Geo. Burton
Mr. John Woodall
Mr. Willm. Fowler
Mr. John Maling
Mr. Robt. Reed.
Mr. Jos. Jewson
Mr. Willm. Coulson
Mr. Willm. Purret
Mr. Willm. Parkin
Mr. Robt. Aclinson
Mr. Geo. Carby
Mr. Thos. Overman
Mr. Robt. Duceberg
Mr. Geo. Sligeholm
Mr. Robt. Foster
Mr. John Marshall
Mr. John Kenyon

Number of Guns Mounted..........99
Number of Persons to Manage the Guns.....400
Number of Persons with small Arms
Quartered at the respective Batterys } 400

Scarborough
A History

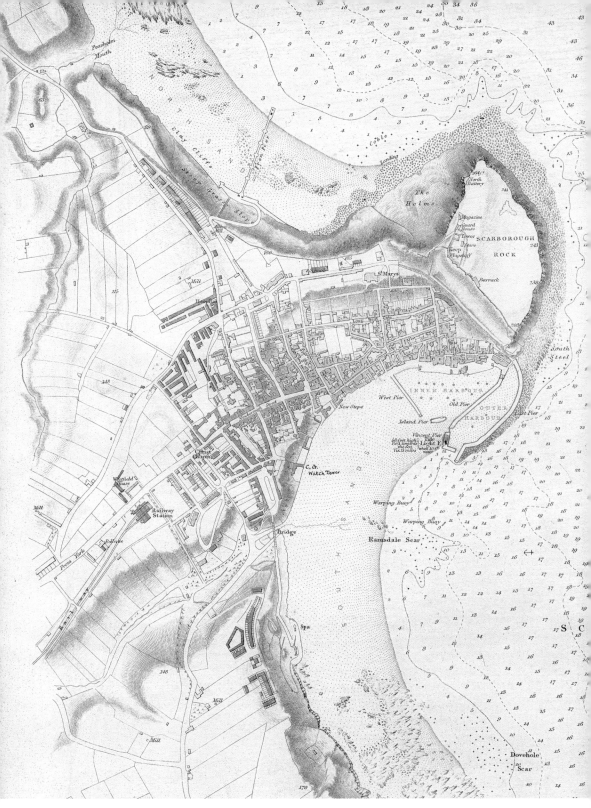

Map of Scarborough surveyed by Master E.K. Calver for the Hydrographic Office of the Admiralty in 1843 with revisions in 1856 and 1871.

SCARBOROUGH
A HISTORY

Trevor Pearson

PHILLIMORE

2009

Published by
PHILLIMORE & CO. LTD
Chichester, West Sussex, England
www.phillimore.co.uk
www.thehistorypress.co.uk

© Trevor Pearson, 2009

ISBN 978-1-86077-568-0

Printed and bound in Great Britain

Contents

To the memory of Robin Shepherd

LIST OF ILLUSTRATIONS

Frontispiece: Map of Scarborough surveyed by Master E.K. Calver for the Hydrographic Office of the Admiralty in 1843 with revisions in 1856 and 1871.

ILLUSTRATION ACKNOWLEDGEMENTS

All the illustrations are by the author or from books, maps and engravings in the author's collection with the following exceptions: British Library, 39; Peter Burton, 30, 42, 140; English Heritage, 1, 7, 11, 14; Chris Hall, 23; David Pearson, 9, 10, 12, 20, 24, 29, 32, 45, 49, 75, 76, 84; Scarborough Archaeological and Historical Society, 28, 31, 41, 149; Scarborough Borough Council, 64 143; Tim Watkins, 26.

Acknowledgements

I first remember becoming aware of Scarborough's past around the time of the millennium celebrations in 1966, when there was much talk of Viking involvement in founding the town. While that now seems to be more myth than reality, there are many other episodes in Scarborough's long history that still excite interest – the prehistoric and Roman periods on the castle headland, the founding of the town in the 12th century, the disastrous sieges in the English Civil War, the discovery of the mineral spring, the birth of the spa and the invention of the modern seaside holiday. Archaeology too has provided many new and interesting discoveries, particularly about the medieval period when Scarborough first rose to prominence as a port. Scarborough is indeed fortunate to have such a rich and varied history. My interest in the history and archaeology of the town has been sustained over many years by Chris and Frances Hall, Jack Binns, Bryan Berryman and John Rushton and by many other friends, past and present, from the Scarborough Archaeological and Historical Society.

In bringing together this historical account of Scarborough I have drawn heavily on previous histories, most notably the 1798 and 1832 editions of Thomas Hinderwell's history of Scarborough, the 1931 volume edited by Arthur Rowntree and the Scarborough Archaeological and Historical Society's 1966 and 2003 publications on the town. The History of Scarborough by Jack Binns, published in 2001, is an invaluable modern reference source for anyone wishing to begin serious research into the history of the town.

1 *The castle headland and Old Town. The headland was first settled at the end of the Bronze Age and was the site of a Roman signal station in the late 4th century A.D.*

_____

ONE

The Earliest Inhabitants: Scarborough Before the Town

Prehistoric Scarborough

The earliest traces of human activity in the Scarborough area are from around 10,000 years ago, soon after the end of the last Ice Age. As the climate slowly warmed, birch, hazel and pine woodland colonised the ice-ravaged lowlands of north-east Yorkshire. Into the woods came the first people; groups of hunter-gatherers following the herds of deer and elk and taking whatever food the woodland plants could provide. At this remote time, called the Mesolithic or Middle Stone Age, the North Sea had yet to form and Scarborough's cliffs and headland formed hills on the edge of a vast lowland plain now referred to as 'Dogger Land', which stretched eastward to the continent. The discovery of bone harpoons and flint tools from under the North Sea shows that Mesolithic people occupied Dogger Land for thousands of years before rising sea levels created the North Sea around eight thousand years ago. Near to Scarborough, archaeologists have found the sites of at least 10 temporary settlements from this period dotted around the eastern end of the Vale of Pickering. The middle of the vale was then a vast lake providing a rich larder of plants, fish and wildfowl and made a sheltered base from which to mount hunting expeditions into the surrounding uplands. These journeys no doubt took them the few miles northwards to the area of the modern town but as yet no discarded flints or other artefacts have been found at Scarborough to prove that these first hunters passed this way.

The groups of Mesolithic hunter-gatherers made little impact on the landscape and the woodland lasted for several thousand years more until the arrival of Neolithic (or New Stone Age) farming communities into this area between around 4000-3000 B.C. The burial mounds of these first agriculturalists, called long barrows, are known from the Wolds to the south of Scarborough and within a few miles of the town to the west along the Tabular Hills, but so far the only trace of them at Scarborough is a number of superbly crafted stone axes found at various sites around the area. The axes would have been used to clear the woodland to create fields and were either lost accidentally or left as ritual offerings. One of the finest of the stone axes from the town was found on the castle dykes on the west side of the headland in 1950. The axe was made of volcanic rock from the Langdale region of the Lake District, over 100

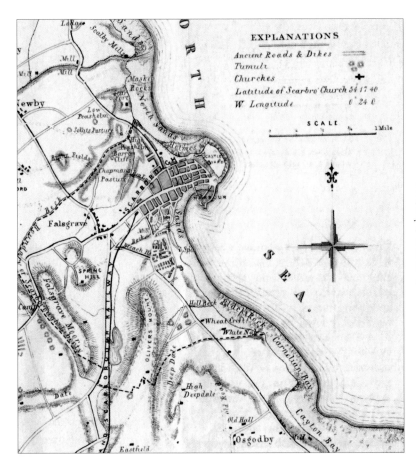

2 *Map of the Scarborough area from the 1850s, showing the sites of many prehistoric burial mounds labelled on the plan as 'Tumuli'.*

miles to the west, and is evidence of the wide-ranging trade contacts of Scarborough's Stone Age farmers.

The introduction of metalworking to this region around 2000 B.C. ushered in the Bronze Age and the archaeological evidence becomes more plentiful. Several large circular burial mounds called round barrows survived until the last century within what is now the built-up area of the town. Dating from around 1500 B.C., several round barrows were situated on the north side above Peasholm Glen, where the hillside was known as 'Barrow Cliff', and there were three burial mounds at Wheatcroft to the south of Scarborough. Almost all trace of these burial mounds was destroyed in the 20th century but pottery vessels and a burial in

a stone cist was found when one of the mounds was opened in 1836.

3 *Engraving of one of the pottery vessels found in the Wheatcroft round barrow in 1835, which contained the ashes of a cremation.*

The most celebrated Bronze Age find from the Scarborough area was made in 1834 in a round barrow close to the cliff edge several miles to the south of the town at Gristhorpe. The mound contained the intact remains of a complete wooden coffin made from the hollowed-out trunk of an oak tree. The previous digs into this and the other burial mounds in the neighbourhood had produced only pottery vessels containing cremations so this discovery was completely unexpected. The landowner, William Beswick, thought at first that the object was an old tree trunk and it was not until the next day as the tree trunk was being dragged out of the mound that the lid fell open to reveal the intact skeleton of a man of above average stature accompanied by a small collection of bronze, bone and flint tools. Mr Beswick donated the coffin and its contents to the recently opened museum of the Philosophical Society in Scarborough (now called the Rotunda Museum). The upsurge in visitors to the museum to see the discovery helped the society pay off the debts left from constructing the building. 'No visitor should leave without taking a peep at his dear departed relative,' urged one Scarborough guide, 'the skeleton, so beautifully preserved, of a British Chieftain of most uncommon stature.'

The round barrow in which the 'Gristhorpe Man' had been interred was built close to the cliff edge to give a commanding view of the ocean, an indication, perhaps, that the sea was not alien to these people. By this period, there were vessels capable of crossing the North Sea, such as the large, plank-sewn boat dating to around 2000 B.C. found on the banks of the Humber at North Ferriby in 1937. At nearly sixteen metres in length, it is estimated that the boat could have accommodated 18 oarsmen and was capable of carrying sizeable cargoes, making it very useful as a coastal trading vessel. Perhaps this is the period when Scarborough's two sandy beaches

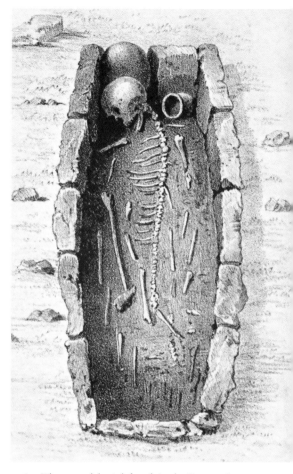

4 *The central burial found in the Bronze Age round barrow at Wheatcroft, excavated in 1835.*

were first used as landing points by seaborne traders, as objects from the period have been found in both bays. A spearhead was found in a construction trench at the bottom of Bland's Cliff in the South Bay in 1956 and a hoard of bronze axes came to light at Scalby Mills in the North Bay in 1916. However, the only evidence of a settlement from this period at Scarborough comes not from either of the bays, but from the headland that divides them.

The settlement dates to near the end of the Bronze Age, around 800-600 B.C., and was found in the 1920s by archaeologists excavating on the cliff top on the east side of the headland.

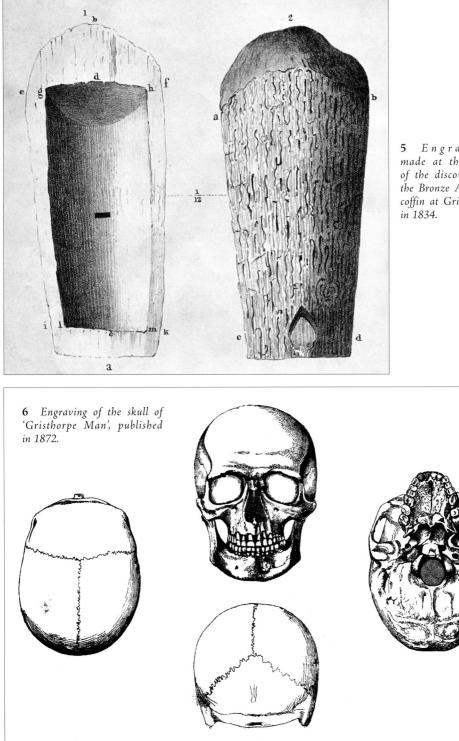

5 *Engraving made at the time of the discovery of the Bronze Age oak coffin at Gristhorpe in 1834.*

6 *Engraving of the skull of 'Gristhorpe Man', published in 1872.*

The dig unearthed 42 rubbish pits containing animal bones and a variety of stone, flint, bone and bronze objects, along with several open-air hearths founded on cobbles. There was evidence for bronze-working and one implement made of iron was found, the earliest recorded use of this metal in the region. The style of some of pottery used on the site closely resembles pottery of the same period from continental Europe around the area of the Lower Rhine. This could indicate that the inhabitants had migrated to the coast of north-east Yorkshire from across the North Sea or, perhaps more likely, that they had trade links with the continent. Either way, the archaeological evidence indicates this was an important settlement whose inhabitants made full use of the North Sea for trade and communication. The discovery of a Late Bronze Age sword during an excavation in 1984 in the middle of the headland suggests that the settlement was more extensive than just the area of the 1920s excavation. More importantly, the discovery of a prestigious object like this sword shows that someone with real wealth and power was associated with the area, the Late Bronze Age equivalent of the medieval lord count William of Aumale, who built the first castle on the same spot 2,000 years later. It is possible too that the settlement was defended by a rampart on the landward side of the headland on approximately the same line as the existing curtain wall of the castle. Protected by high cliffs on the other sides, a rampart would have turned the headland into an almost impregnable hill fort that would have dominated the surrounding area in much the same way as the later castle. The idea of the hill fort at Scarborough is pure speculation and, whether it is true or not, the settlement disappeared by about 600 B.C. After that, the headland seems to have been deserted for almost a thousand years until very near the end of the Roman period.

The Romans at Scarborough

The Roman period in north-east Yorkshire began in A.D. 71 when the Roman army crossed the River Humber and established the legionary fortress at York. Other forts were established around the region but the coast was left unprotected until the end of the Roman occupation was approaching. Then, around A.D. 370, the headland at Scarborough was chosen as the location for one of a chain of signal stations along the coast of north-east Yorkshire whose purpose was to warn of incursions by seaborne raiders from the north of Britain and the continent. The Scarborough signal station was discovered in the 1920s on the edge of the east cliff on the same site as the Late Bronze Age discoveries. Although about a quarter of the signal station has been lost due to the erosion of the cliff edge, it clearly followed the same plan as the other stations in the chain. In essence, each of the signal stations was a heavily fortified watchtower laid out on a broadly square-shaped plan. The outer defences consisted of a deep, V-shaped ditch with a curtain wall behind. This enclosed a courtyard at the centre of which stood a tower several floors high. There is still no agreement as to how high the tower stood, but some estimates make it as high as the keep of the medieval castle. From this vantage point the garrison of perhaps no more than 30 men could keep a lookout to sea for any sign of raids. Although the coast itself was not heavily settled at this time, inland was one of the richest farming areas in the North of England with numerous farmsteads in the Vale of Pickering and across the Tabular Hills to the west, while further south on the Wolds there were several very wealthy estates with large villa residences. The signal stations would have made an impressive sight dotted along the coast on prominent cliffs and headlands and their very presence undoubtedly deterred some raiding parties. When needed

7   *Reconstruction painting of the Roman signal station at Scarborough.*

though, reinforcements could be dispatched to the coast from the nearest Roman fort at Malton, 20 miles inland, or from the legionary headquarters at York. However these defences lasted for no more than 40 years. Roman power collapsed in Britain in A.D. 410 and the signal stations were abandoned to their fate.

The signal station is not the only evidence that the Romans were at Scarborough. Quite a few coins have come from the harbour, suggesting the Romans made use of the sheltered anchorage provided by the South Bay, and Castle Road may perpetuate the line of a Roman route heading along the north cliff on to the headland to the signal station. Near Castle Road traces have been found of a possible Roman farming settlement. The Roman remains were found preserved below the rampart of the later medieval town defences on a building site at the north end of St Thomas Street in 1999. Among the finds were part of a Roman quern stone for the grinding

of cereals and fragments of pottery from the third century A.D.

Anglo-Saxon and Viking Settlement

With the abandonment of the Roman signal station Scarborough enters into a true Dark Age with no written or archaeological evidence for several centuries. The coastal area was very probably settled by Anglo-Saxons in the fifth and sixth centuries. These people were the descendents of the seaborne raiders that had so troubled the Romans along the Yorkshire coast in the fourth century A.D. They came from the coastal regions of Denmark and northern Germany and migrated across the North Sea in considerable numbers after the collapse of Roman authority. The groups of settlers eventually came together to create the Anglo-Saxon kingdom of Deira in the early seventh century, centred upon the former Roman legionary fortress and civil settlement of York. It is the Anglo-Saxons who are believed to have first started to use the name

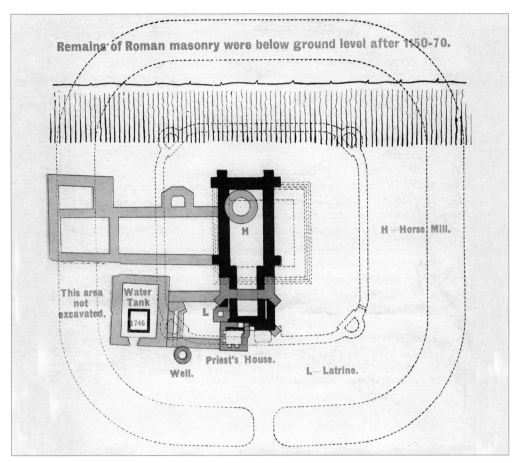

Remains of Roman masonry were below ground level after 1150-70.

H – Horse Mill.

This area not excavated.

Water Tank

1746

L

Well.

Priest's House.

L – Latrine.

8 *The plan of the Roman and medieval discoveries made on the castle headland between 1919 and 1925. The ditch, curtain wall and central tower of the Roman signal station is shown in outline overlain by later buildings including a medieval chapel.*

'Scarborough', giving the name to the headland rather than to an actual settlement. The name means 'the hill with the fort' and is a perfect description of the headland with the Roman signal station, which would still have been a significant landmark when the Anglo-Saxons arrived despite having been long abandoned.

Following on from the Anglo-Saxons of the fifth and sixth centuries came the Vikings in the ninth and 10th centuries, firstly as marauders and later as settlers. Most came from Denmark and the distribution of village names ending in 'by' or 'thorpe' shows that the Danes settled locally around the Vale of Pickering and along the coastal strip inland from Scarborough at villages with

names such as Newby, Throxenby, Osgodby and Gristhorpe. But what of Scarborough itself?

A seafaring people like the Vikings would surely have taken advantage of a site like Scarborough, with its naturally sheltered anchorage and the prominent landmark created by the headland. It is therefore no surprise to find Scarborough mentioned in several saga stories from the Viking era and these create the impression that Scarborough was an important place to them in the 10th and 11th centuries. The earliest mention is in Kormak's Saga, which relates how two brothers called Kormak and Thorgils Skardi, leaders of a band of Icelandic warriors, built a fort on this part of the coast

9 *The saga account of the burning of Scarborough in 1066 places the settlement immediately below the headland near to the harbour. No remains of it have been found by archaeologists.*

10 *Reconstruction of the Norwegian attack of 1066 and the burning of Scarborough.*

around the year 966 that got the name 'Scardi's Burgh', meaning Skardi's fort. This was long believed to be the origin of the name Scarborough and the most likely location of Thorgil's fort would have been the ruined Roman signal station on the headland. However, no remains of any Viking fortification were found when the signal station was excavated and, as was mentioned earlier, it is now thought that the name Scarborough is Anglo-Saxon and therefore was in use long before the Vikings arrived off the coast of north-east Yorkshire. Sadly, it seems that Thorgils Skardi and his fort may be nothing more than a colourful story, but nevertheless one that Scarborough can still be proud of.

In the following century Scarborough appears briefly in several sagas recounting the exploits of King Harald Hardrada of Norway and his attempt to capture the English throne in the autumn of 1066. The king sailed with a fleet of some 300 ships from the Orkney Isles aiming for the Humber Estuary and the route up the River Ouse to York. During the voyage south the sagas mention that the Norwegian invasion fleet landed at Scarborough and set fire to a settlement they describe as a town. The most detailed description of these events is preserved in the Heimskringla Saga compiled by the Icelandic poet Snorri Sturluson in the early 13th century. He tells of how the Norwegians met fierce resistance from the townsfolk after they landed and so resorted to building a large bonfire on the hill above the town. Once it was aflame they pushed the burning embers down onto the buildings below and so forced the surrender of the town. Scarborough had its revenge a few short weeks later when King Harald Hardrada and most of his army were killed fighting the English forces at the Battle of Stamford Bridge, a few miles to the east of York.

The saga account of the events at Scarborough creates a vivid picture of a town of simple wooden houses nestling at the foot of the headland with a bonfire blazing on the summit above. The area of the modern town nearest to the headland - Quay Street, Burr Bank and Castlegate - would seem to be the right sort of area for the settlement destroyed in 1066. However, despite archaeological excavations in several places along these streets, no trace of any settlement from 1066 has ever been found – not even one scrap of pottery or a single post hole from a building. In 1066 the area below the headland seems to have been open, unoccupied ground, so why is there a description of a town in the Heimskringla? The most likely explanation is that the Snorri Sturluson based his account on the town that existed in his day, in the early 13th century, which did indeed start at the foot of the headland and spread inland around the South Bay. It was his mistake, but he had no way of knowing that this town actually dated back less than 100 years and therefore had not existed at the time of the Norwegian invasion in 1066.

The only archaeological finds at Scarborough from the time of the Viking settlements come from the headland, where archaeologists in the 1920s found traces of a small rectangular chapel built within the ruins of the central tower of the Roman signal station. The chapel had a small graveyard containing the remains of men, women and children buried around the year A.D. 1000. In this period the largest settlement in the district was not on the coast but a mile or so inland at Falsgrave. This village was a royal manor with jurisdiction over most neighbouring villages from Staintondale in the north to Filey in the south and inland as far as Brompton. The inhabitants of Falsgrave may have been responsible for founding the chapel and graveyard on the headland, but exactly when or why still remains to be discovered. There is no mention of the chapel or of a place called Scarborough in the Domesday survey. This omission has been used as evidence that Scarborough was wiped off the face of the map in the Norwegian invasion of 1066, but a more likely reason is that those sent to assess the wealth of the area for William the Conqueror found nothing on this part of the coast of any value worth noting.

Two

Scarborough in the Middle Ages

The Founding of Scarborough

In the hundred years after Domesday, Scarborough rose from obscurity to become one of the most important towns in the North of England, the site of a royal castle and a port that was among the largest on the East Coast. The transformation of what up until the 12th century was a remote and sparsely populated stretch of coastline began around the year 1138 with the construction of the first castle on the headland by count William of Aumale, lord of the Holderness region of eastern Yorkshire. History has not been kind to the reputation of count William of Aumale. He emerges from the chronicles of the time as a physically grotesque human being, so fat that he was unable to ride a horse and so repulsive that his wife left him soon after their marriage. He sacked Selby Abbey, laid waste villages for a hunting reserve and tried to manipulate the election of the Archbishop of York for his own ends. But Scarborough should have a kinder view of him. By constructing a castle on the headland he kick-started the process that led within a few decades to Scarborough becoming one of the largest towns in Yorkshire.

No buildings now survive from this period, but it is thought that count William of Aumale's castle would have been constructed largely of timber and probably occupied roughly the same area as the inner bailey of the later castle. At its heart was a tower referred to by a later chronicler as 'a very costly work', and here count William of Aumale would have maintained a garrison to exert his authority over this stretch of the coast. It seems that the security afforded by the new castle attracted people to settle at Scarborough. The documentary references are scant but sufficient to indicate that a small fishing and trading community came into existence in the 15 or so years that count William of Aumale held Scarborough. In the late 1140s Ranulf, earl of Chester, seized a fisherman at Scarborough and in 1153 the King of Norway seized vessels and property. A settlement had started to grow and probably clustered near present-day West Sandgate, where a now-vanished stream called variously the Damgeth, Damyet or Damyot in the medieval period cut through the cliff to provide fresh water and a natural route down onto the South Bay beach. Higher up the slope there

11 *Count William of Aumale's timber tower was probably in the same area as the later stone keep of Henry II.*

may have been a second settlement immediately outside the gates of count William of Aumale's castle along the approach to the headland. The medieval parish church of St Mary's stands here and could have been founded in this period by count William.

Count William of Aumale was not to continue to enjoy the political and economic benefits of holding the castle and harbour at Scarborough because in 1155 he was forced to surrender the castle to the Crown. His problem was that Scarborough had never been his to build on but was part of the ancient, pre-conquest royal manor of Falsgrave. This had not mattered when count William of Aumale built the castle in the 1130s because royal authority had been weak and the country was racked by civil war. This all

changed late in 1154 when Henry II was crowned King of England. He immediately came north to assert the authority of the throne and at a meeting in York in early 1155 he forced count William of Aumale to surrender his possessions to the Crown, chief among which was the castle at Scarborough.

This was to prove a fortunate turn of events for the fledgling settlement and port at Scarborough. Instead of abandoning the castle and letting Scarborough wither away, Henry II chose instead to rebuild it along much stronger lines. In the space of a few years he turned count William of Aumale's castle from a fairly minor timber fortification to an impregnable royal fortress. Beginning in 1158, it took 10 years to complete the new castle. At its heart stood an

12 *Reconstruction painting of the possible settlement on the route to the count of Aumale's castle, which is seen in the background on the headland.*

impressive 100ft-high stone keep that dominated the two bays and was visible for miles along the coast. With walls 30ft thick, most of the building stands to this day so it is possible to explore the interior and see how it was divided into various rooms across several levels, beginning with store rooms and a great hall on the ground and first floors to private rooms for the castle governor and his retainers towards the top of the building. The keep sits within an inner bailey that was also completed by Henry II and dominates the only route up from the town onto the headland, now marked by a line of later medieval defences and an outer gatehouse constructed some 200 years after the keep.

Scarborough Castle helped stamp Henry's dominance over the region, a symbol of a personal empire that stretched from the Scottish borders to the Pyrenees by the end of his reign in 1189. Unfortunately there is no evidence that such an important figure in medieval history actually came to Scarborough to see the site himself, but a visit to the coast after his meeting with count William in York may explain why he took the decision to rebuild the castle and create a new town at Scarborough.

The Town

Whatever settlement existed when Scarborough was controlled by count William of Aumale was completely transformed by Henry II, who ordered the laying out of a new town beyond the castle headland which he then favoured with the grant of a royal charter of privileges

13 *Henry II's stone keep, constructed between 1158 and 1168.*

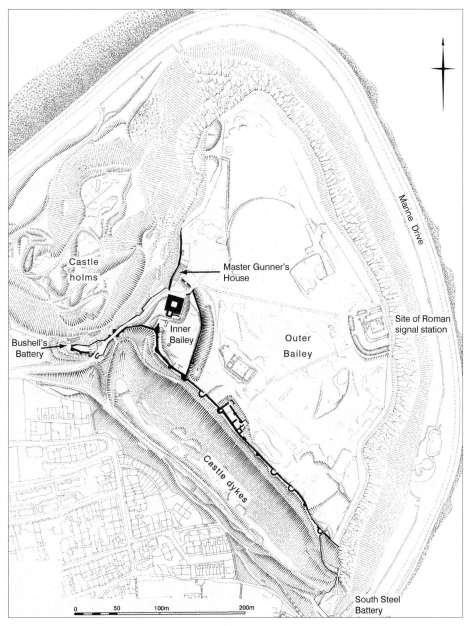

14 *Plan of the headland showing the main elements of the medieval castle and earthworks.*

sometime before the year 1163. The charter elevated the new settlement to the status of a royal borough, which gave its inhabitants the freedom to trade and associate beyond anything enjoyed by the rural population at this time. It also set out the arrangements for the payment of tax to the royal exchequer, for ultimately

Henry's interest in fostering the development of the town was to feed revenue back into the royal coffers. The same motivation lay behind the creation of many new towns in England during the 12th and 13th centuries, not only by the Crown but also by the Church and nobility as well. In 1158 the first payment of £22 from

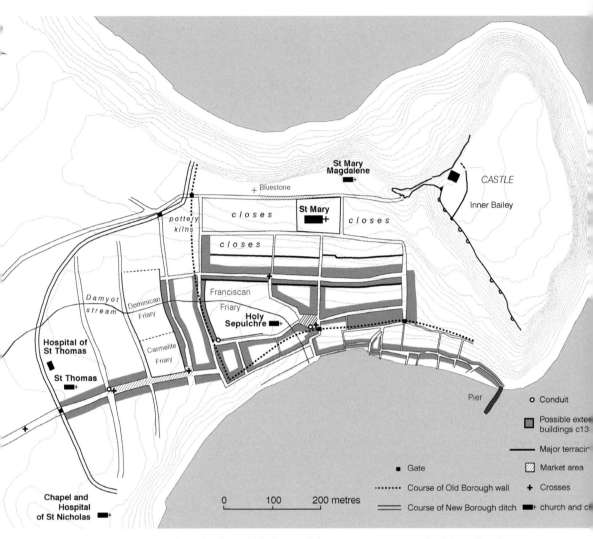

15 *Plan of medieval Scarborough. The grid-like layout of the streets seen across much of the medieval town is evidence that the Old and New Boroughs were planned when they were created in the reign of Henry II.*

Scarborough reached the exchequer but by the end of Henry's reign in 1189 the amount paid had increased to over £60, testament to the rapid expansion in the prosperity of the town in the first decades of its existence. It was a scale of growth that proved impossible to sustain in following centuries.

By the end of Henry's reign the town covered an area of more than 80 acres, well over twice that of the castle and headland. The new town developed in two main stages, with the establishment first of the Old Borough, which started at the foot of the castle headland and spread inland for a distance of about five hundred metres. It occupied all the ground between the cliffs overlooking the North and South Bays and ended in the west at a defensive wall and ditch facing inland. The ditch was around thirty-five feet wide and some 15ft deep when originally constructed and, with a rampart and stone wall to its rear, created an impressive barrier communicating Scarborough's status as

16 *The ditch on the north side of the New Borough survived as a water-filled hollow into the 1820s called the New Dyke. Engraving by Francis Nicholson.*

a royal borough. There is some evidence that the wall continued along the south side of the Old Borough following a line back to the foot of the castle headland along the crest of the low cliff overlooking the South Bay.

The creation of the Old Borough took the early part of Henry's reign to complete but then, in the 1170s or early 1180s, the town almost doubled in size with the creation of the New Borough outside the western wall of the Old Borough. The New Borough ended in the west at a line later defined by defences stretching from modern-day St Nicholas Cliff on the south along Bar Street and North Street that then curved eastwards to join with the Old Borough defences. This defensive boundary continued to define the built-up area of the town until close to the end of the 18th century.

The only building in the town to have survived from this period is the parish church of St Mary's, which includes fabric thought to date from the 1180s soon after work had been completed on the castle keep. The church is almost as dominant as the castle keep occupying a ridge-top site near to the main entrance to the castle from where most of the old town is clearly visible. The considerable income that came to the parish church from tithes on the sale of fish at Scarborough was given by Henry's successor, Richard I, in 1189 to the Cistercians, an order of monks with over 500 houses in Europe, most of them in France but including Rievaulx Abbey, Byland Abbey and Fountains Abbey in Yorkshire. So lucrative was this grant to the Cistercian order that in the following century they established a small community of monks in the town under the leadership of a Proctor to oversee more closely the revenues of the parish church, leading to the mistaken idea among early historians of the town that there had been a Cistercian abbey at Scarborough.

The idea in creating a new town on such an enormous scale was to accommodate a rapidly growing population attracted to Scarborough

17   *A watercolour from the early 1800s of the New Dyke.*

by the opportunity for trade, the protection of the new royal castle and, most importantly, by the expansion of a port in the South Bay. Scarborough was a naturally safe anchorage with its wide sandy beach and the protection from the worst of the elements afforded by the mass of the castle headland. Count William of Aumale appreciated this and may have started the development of the harbour but real expansion only came later in the century with the rapid and widespread growth in the volume of seaborne trade along the East Coast that came with more settled times. The harbour at this early period was probably nothing more sophisticated than a series of paved slipways and timber jetties stretching along the high-water mark between the headland and modern-day West Sandgate, where the small vessels of this period could berth and be pulled up on to the beach for unloading. The majority of these vessels would have been

from the town's own fishing fleet because much of Scarborough's early prosperity was built on profits from the herring fishery. The catches were sold at a market on the beach to traders that included many of the newly founded religious houses in north-east Yorkshire, including the Cistercian monasteries of Rievaulx, Byland and Fountains and the Gilbertine priory at Malton. Each of these houses owned property in Scarborough by the end of the 12th century as their interests in the port increased.

Few records exist of the families who first settled in the new town of Scarborough in the 12th century. From what has survived it seems that two or three families initially dominated the town, buying up many of the house plots to become the landlords of those who came later. Chief among this small group of landlords was the Uctred family, one of whose descendents in the late 13th century is recorded as holding an

18 *St Mary's Church in the 19th century. The church occupies a dominant position on the ridge top near the castle entrance and may date back to the time of the first castle built by count William of Aumale in the 12th century.*

19 *St Mary's Church as it must have appeared towards the end of the Middle Ages. The two impressive towers at the west end were taken down in the middle of the 16th century after suffering storm damage.*

20   *Reconstruction painting of Cook's Row in the Old Borough in the late Middle Ages. In the background is the tower of the chapel of the Holy Sepulchre.*

21   *The timber-framed house at 2 Quay Street is one of only a handful of domestic buildings to survive from the medieval town.*

estate of over 80 properties for rent in the town, making him one of Scarborough's wealthiest inhabitants. The houses that the Uctred family rented out in Scarborough in the 12th century would have been simple single-storey buildings constructed of wood with thatch roofs fronting on to the street, with extensive yards to the rear. Those involved in fishing would have used the yards for repairing nets and drying fish, while others would have earned their living from crafts such as bone and leather-working or used their properties to sell food or household goods. Baxtergate, meaning the street of the bakers, is one of the earliest recorded names in Scarborough, occurring in documents as early as the 1170s. However, the name has not survived to modern times. Around the harbour some houses were built of stone, probably by merchants, in order to withstand the ravages of the sea at a period when there was no waterfront to speak of and also to display the wealth of

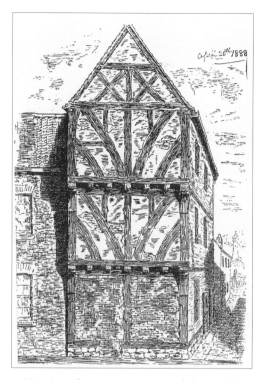

22 *A 19th-century engraving of the possibly medieval timber-framed building at 25 Quay Street, which was taken down in 1964.*

23 *The timber framing at 9 Leading Post Street was only discovered in 2003. It may date to the late 15th century.*

their owners. No stone houses from this early period have survived, but they probably included a cellar where goods could be stored prior to transshipment through the port and would have been several storeys high, making them the largest private dwellings in the town.

In the middle of the 13th century King Henry III bestowed a wide range of new legal and economic privileges on the town in a group of charters dated between 1253 and 1256. That Scarborough needed this help from the Crown testifies to the struggle the town faced in the 13th century to maintain the gains of the previous century. Then, Scarborough had been the only port of note along the Yorkshire coast but a century later ports such as Whitby, Bridlington and Ravenser at the mouth of the Humber Estuary were drawing trade away from Scarborough. Scarborough received the right to

hold a 40-day fair in the charter of 1256, to be held annually in the late summer. This coincided with the period when the herring shoals were off the coast and the fair therefore encouraged the landing and processing of fish at Scarborough. The town also served as a local market for the sale of livestock and agricultural produce. There were market places in the Old Borough at the east end of St Sepulchre Street marked by the Butter Cross and along Castle Road where, according to tradition, the Bluestone, now in the care of the museum, was where the bargains were struck. In the New Borough, the wide main street, now called Newborough, served as the market place. Scarborough faced fierce competition as a market centre from local villages, most notably Seamer, situated several miles to the south of Scarborough at the eastern end of the Vale of Pickering. With good communications routes

24 *The rear of the Lancaster Inn in Quay Street. Research indicates that the timber-framing preserved in the Three Mariners House, seen in the photograph further down the street, originally belonged to one large late-medieval building.*

around the vale, Seamer was better placed than Scarborough to act as a local market centre but the charter of 1256 prohibited the development of a market both there and at other nearby villages to protect Scarborough's. A second royal charter in 1256 extended the borough boundary to include the manor of Falsgrave and this was another important step in securing the prosperity of Scarborough. As a consequence of this grant the town received some 60 acres of arable land scattered among the fields of Falsgrave to enable it to broaden its economic

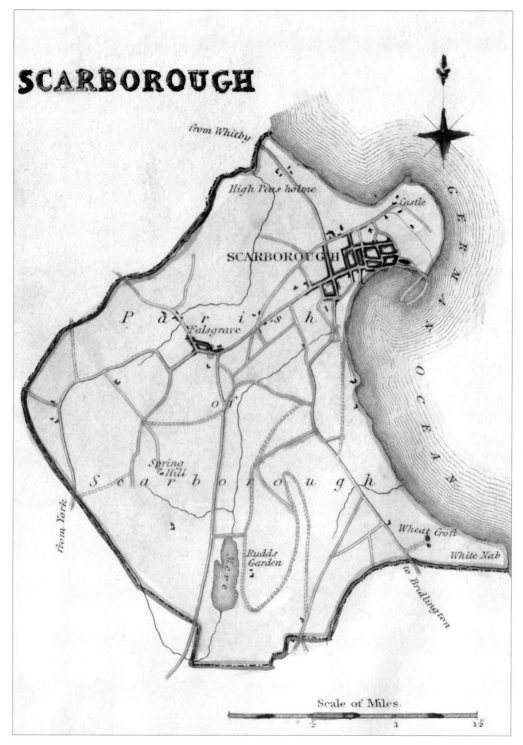

25 *A map from the 1830s showing the boundary of Scarborough established after the charter of 1256.*

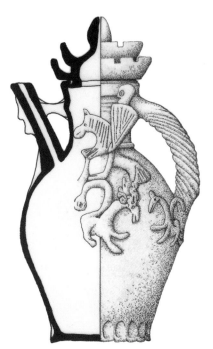

26   *Drawing of a Scarborough Ware 'knight jug'.*

base by extending its role as an agricultural centre. The charters show that Scarborough's period of rapid growth and prosperity was over but, equally, they were sufficiently generous and wide-ranging to secure the town's future a century after its foundation.

The Later Middle Ages

As Scarborough moved past the middle of the 13th century, the number and variety of documents relating to the town increases so that, by the 14th century, we get our clearest picture yet of the character of the town, a century and a half after its foundation. Archaeological discoveries made in recent years also contribute to the picture of Scarborough in the later Middle Ages.

The physical distinction between the Old and New Boroughs, so important as early stages in the town's development, gradually disappeared as the Middle Ages wore on. By the 14th century the wall and ditch that separated them had largely disappeared, the wall becoming a suitable quarry

for stone or being incorporated in buildings, while the ditch became filled with rubbish. So thoroughly did these defences disappear that their exact course was lost until the ditch was unexpectedly discovered by local archaeologists on two sites bordering Leading Post Street on what had been the south-west corner of the Old Borough in the late 1980s. Sufficient deeds and other property records survive from the 14th century to show that large parts of the medieval town within the defences, particularly to the north, were left as open, unoccupied ground divided into small fields and paddocks rather than house plots. It seems that 150 years on from the establishment of the town, Scarborough had failed to attract the size of population anticipated when the Old and New Boroughs were laid out by Henry II. In contrast, other streets in the south of the Old Borough and around the market place in the New Borough were crowded with houses, as was the foreshore between the foot of the castle headland and West Sandgate. Properties here commanded the highest rents of anywhere in the town as fishermen, merchants and craftsmen vied with each other to be near the economic heart of the town around the harbour.

The archaeological and documentary sources come together to show that the pressure for building land around the harbour led to a massive programme of land reclamation beginning in earnest after the 1253 charter, in which the Crown decreed that Scarborough should have the money to create 'a new port' where vessels could berth at both high and low tides. This necessitated creating a new harbour front further out into the waters of the South Bay to obtain deeper water and provide more space for building by consolidating the land to the rear. Once started, the process of building out into the harbour continued in a piecemeal fashion throughout the remainder of the Middle Ages.

Archaeological evidence of this reclamation process has come to light in several excavations in the foreshore in the form of thick deposits of decaying household refuse from the 14th and 15th centuries, which were deliberately dumped behind the waterfront to level up the ground for building. Elsewhere around the harbour, development out into the South Bay took place where there were natural dune-like accumulations of beach sand, referred to in 15th-century documents as the Sandhills.

The efforts made by the town to maintain and develop the waterfront were crucial if the town was to maintain its widespread trading links with other East Coast ports as well as from the continent, particularly the Low Countries and the Baltic. The town's own fishing fleet also needed to have a serviceable waterfront where catches could be unloaded. This fleet numbered around ten vessels in 1312. Aside from fish, the main goods traded through the port at the beginning of the 14th century were timber from the Baltic and agricultural produce from the countryside around Scarborough, which was traded to other East Coast ports. Pottery was also exported from the town from kilns situated in the north of the Old Borough along Castle Road. The kilns were active from at least the middle of the 13th century to well into the 14th century, producing tableware covered in a lustrous green glaze and more specialised and highly decorated vessels called knight jugs decorated with representations of a knight carrying a shield. Referred to by archaeologists as Scarborough Ware, sherds of the pottery are found in excavations in ports right along the East Coast of England and Scotland and occasionally on the continent from the north of France to southern Scandinavia, Iceland and the Baltic. This distribution, recovered through archaeological research, is therefore a useful indication of the town's far-reaching trade links at the height of the Middle Ages.

With the greater abundance of documentary sources after the middle of the 13th century we get a clearer picture of the religious life of the town. The parish church of St Mary's had two dependent chapels in the town, the chapel of the Holy Sepulchre in the Old Borough and the chapel of St Thomas in the New Borough. The foundation date of both chapels is not known precisely but it is possible that they date back to the 12th century. The chapel of the Holy Sepulchre, which stood near to West Sandgate and is commemorated by the name of St Sepulchre Street, may date back to the period of count William and point to an area of settlement pre-dating the establishment of the Old Borough by Henry II. The chapel of St Thomas stood at the western edge of the New Borough on a slight eminence overlooking the borough's central market street. Beyond the town, a leper hospital and chapel dedicated to St Nicholas stood on the edge of the cliff overlooking the South Bay, about where the *Grand Hotel* stands today on St Nicholas Cliff.

Between the middle of the 13th century and the early 14th century these chapels were joined by new religious establishments as three orders of friars each established houses in the town. The Dominicans were the first to settle permanently

27 *Engraving of a medieval copper plate from a coffin found on the site of the chapel and hospital of St Nicholas in 1810.*

in Scarborough, establishing an extensive friary on vacant land between Queen Street and Cross Street in the north of the New Borough in 1252. The Franciscans settled next in 1267, establishing a friary in the heart of the Old Borough on what was an unoccupied, marshy tract of land crossed by the Damyet stream to the west of the chapel of the Holy Sepulchre. In 1319 the Carmelite friars settled, establishing a friary in the New Borough between the Dominican friary and the central market street.

That the town was able to support three friaries as well as the parish church and its dependent chapels is one measure of the wealth

28 *In the Middle Ages the Franciscans in the Old Borough canalised the Damyet stream where it crossed the grounds of their friary. This section was discovered in an archaeological excavation in 1997.*

its trading activities generated. Another is the amount of tax that the town paid in the assessments of 1312 and 1377, which placed it among the 30 wealthiest towns in the country. However, despite the economic strength of the town, there was little visible sign of its wealth. No lavish and impressive civic buildings were constructed and no money was forthcoming to build prestigious gates at the entry points into the town or walls to defend it. Nor have any rich objects such as expensive imported pottery or fine metalwork come to light on archaeological excavations. The general level of the material culture of the town appears to have been quite poor, suggesting there was a big divide between the mass of the citizenry who lived in poverty and a small group of wealthy elite who controlled most of the revenues of the town whether through rent, trade or control of the fishing fleet. Members of this same group of elite families formed the council that ran the town and periodically elected two or three bailiffs from among its own numbers to exercise executive control over the town's affairs. Anger at the exploitative nature of this closed system of town government flared into open rebellion in June 1381 at the height of the so-called Peasants' Revolt. Although the Peasants' Revolt was focussed upon London and the South, discontent also flared up in Scarborough and was aimed chiefly at one of the two bailiffs, Robert Acclom, who, although meant to be the servant of the town, had for years past used his position to extort money from the townsfolk and plunder their goods and chattels. Spurred on by events in the South of the country, a 500-strong force of rebel townsfolk laid siege to Acclom's house in Scarborough and those of his associates, who sought refuge at the Franciscan friary and the parish church. After a stand-off lasting several days the rebels secured promises from Acclom and his associates that they would recompense the town for all their past misdeeds, but after order returned and the rebels dispersed all the historical evidence suggests Acclom continued in his abuses.

While the corruption and abuses practised by Acclom were exceptionally bad, Scarborough most probably suffered throughout the Middle Ages from the self-serving interests of its principal families. As one dynasty faded away so others rose to perpetuate the abuses against the town. Indeed, it was left to the Franciscan friars to undertake the greatest civic improvements of the later Middle Ages when they organised the construction of a piped water supply from springs a mile inland at the village of Falsgrave in 1319. The water was conveyed to the town in a stone channel and distributed at three conduits situated at the east end of the New Borough market street, and in the Old Borough at either end of St Sepulchre Street. Before this great act of benefaction, the townsfolk were forced to obtain their water from private wells or from the borough well situated in the Old Borough

at the east end of St Sepulchre Street.

The addition of four side chapels on the south side of the parish church at the end of the 14th century and the rebuilding of the eastern chancel of the church in the mid-15th century is evidence of the wealth that some citizens had available to pass on to the parish church. Very little now survives of the chancel due to the damage it suffered in the 17th century during the English Civil War and later stone-robbing, but evidence points to it being ornately decorated, with two side aisles and a magnificent east window looking towards the castle headland.

Expenditure on the castle tailed off considerably during the later Middle Ages as it became an outdated symbol of royal authority. Henry III was the last monarch to spend lavishly on the fortifications in the 13th century, creating an elaborate and heavily fortified entrance with a central tower and drawbridges on either side spanning the defile that cut across the neck of the promontory between the castle dykes and the North Bay cliffs. Further defences were

29 *The south side of St Mary's Church, showing two of the late medieval side chapels.*

throne. While still duke of Gloucester Richard had visited Scarborough several times in his role as admiral of the North and, after succeeding to the throne in 1483, he spent money to secure Scarborough as his main naval base in the North. This meant finding more money to repair the waterfront and also making a start on building a wall around the western side of the town to strengthen the old ditch and rampart. A short stretch of this wall still survives in the north of the medieval New Borough facing on to Castle Road. It is built of neatly coursed blocks standing on the levelled base of the earlier rampart. Archaeological excavations have shown that the wall lacked foundations and was barely a couple of feet thick, suggesting it was built

30   *King Richard III, as portrayed by Mr Eliot Nelson in the Scarborough pageant of 1912.*

added in the middle of the 14th century with the construction of a barbican beyond Henry's drawbridges. Triangular in plan and much restored, the barbican still serves as the entrance to the castle while Henry III's two drawbridges were replaced by stone bridges in the 19th century. Despite these two episodes of building in the 13th and 14th centuries, the Crown failed to keep up maintenance and government records contain the results of several surveys highlighting the poor state of repair.

For a brief period towards the end of the 15th century there seemed some hope that Scarborough's gradual decline might be suddenly reversed with the accession of Richard III to the

31   *In 1996 an archaeological excavation at the north end of St Thomas Street found that the last upstanding section of Richard III's town wall rested on the top of the earlier town rampart.*

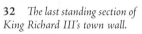

32 *The last standing section of King Richard III's town wall.*

33 *The wooden drawbridge on the exterior of Henry III's gate tower depicted in the early 19th century.*

more for show than to provide Scarborough with a formidable defence, which by this date would have had to have been able to withstand artillery bombardment. The earliest view of Scarborough, believed to date from 1539, shows sections of wall flanking the two entrances into the town at Auborough Gate on the north and Newborough Gate on the west, indicating that the wall was unfinished when Richard III was killed at the Battle of Bosworth Field in 1485 and the money dried up. Alternatively, if the wall was erected only for show then maybe the intention only ever had been to construct short lengths of wall flanking the gates so as to create an impressive sight on entering the town. The 1539 view shows the ditch in front of the Newborough Gate full of water, which again may have been less for defence or the result of uncontrolled flooding as to enhance the setting of the main entrance into the town.

34 *The stone-built house on Sandside is traditionally known as Richard III House, from the belief that it was the King's residence when in Scarborough. Recent research indicates it was probably built in the 17th century.*

THREE

Scarborough in the 16th Century

Richard III's death at the Battle of Bosworth Field in 1485 brought the first of the Tudor dynasty, Henry VII, to the throne. Throughout the 16th century the Tudors showed little interest in either the town or the castle except in times of war and rebellion, when Scarborough's strategic importance as a port once again placed it on the national stage. The accession of Henry VII ushered in a period of steady economic decline that continued throughout the 16th century as the town fought a continuous battle to maintain the profitability of its markets and fishing fleet and the physical structure of the port.

Scarborough was propelled onto the national stage in the reign of Henry VIII in the autumn of 1536 when the town and castle were caught up in the Northern rebellion called the Pilgrimage of Grace. The main cause of the rebellion was dissatisfaction with Henry's split with Rome and his decision to dissolve the monasteries and other religious houses, bringing centuries of established religious practice and devotion to an abrupt end. The changes led to an open rebellion in the North of England against the reforms, led by a minor nobleman from the West Riding called Robert Aske. The capture of Scarborough Castle became one of the objectives of the rebels and the governor, Sir Ralph Eure

the younger, whose family held land at Ayton, a few miles inland from Scarborough, was forced to defend Scarborough against a group of rebels drawn mainly from disaffected country folk from East Riding villages. It is said that Sir Ralph and his small garrison were besieged by the rebels for 20 days, during which time they only had bread and water to sustain them. The rebels are reputed to have brought artillery to bear against the walls of the castle, destroying 75 yards of the curtain wall on the north side overlooking the castle holms. The destruction failed to secure the surrender of the castle but, if true, it was a small foretaste of the much greater destruction that was to befall the castle a century later in the English Civil War. More likely though is that the wall had been left to decay and the siege was used as an excuse to obtain money from the Crown for repairs after the rebellion had been suppressed.

The importance of Scarborough to the rebels in the Pilgrimage of Grace served to alert the Crown to the continued strategic importance of this decaying medieval fortress and the King received two written surveys of the state of the castle soon after. The first, by the governor Sir Ralph Eure, hid the fact that he himself had despoiled the fabric for financial reward

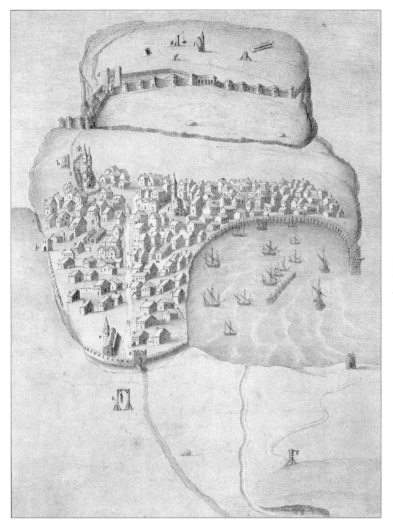

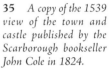

35 *A copy of the 1539 view of the town and castle published by the Scarborough bookseller John Cole in 1824.*

by stripping the lead of various roofs to make a brewing vessel for use at his house at Foulbridge, near Pickering. The second, more detailed survey was compiled in 1538 by Sir Ralph Ellerker and Sir Marmaduke Constable and contains a wealth of detail about the poor physical condition of the castle. The survey they submitted to Henry VIII mentioned the need to repair 37 yards of walling at the outer gatehouse with stone from the castle cliff; that the gate into the inner bailey (which no longer survives) required half a ton of iron for hooks, nails and bands to repair it; while 40 tons of wood was needed to replace

rotten and decaying timbers in the keep. With the Tudor taste for palaces and comfortable living, the castle's days as a royal residence had clearly long since passed.

Nothing had been done to improve the defences of the castle when the building threat of an invasion from continental Europe led the King's chief minister, Thomas Cromwell, to undertake an urgent survey of the state of coastal defences early in 1539. In February he issued an order instructing 'expert men in every shire to view the places along the sea coast where any danger of invasion is likely to be'. For easy

36   *Enlargement of the 1824 engraving of Scarborough in 1539, showing the castle defences.*

assimilation the information was sent to London in the form of sketch plans for Henry himself to scrutinise, and so Scarborough has this invasion scare to thank for the creation of the earliest view of the town, which may date from March 1539, a month after Cromwell's order was issued. Sadly, there is no record of who compiled this sketch view though one of Hull prepared at the same time was by the same hand. As large as a modern A2 sheet of paper, the sketch is delivered in a bold pen with the addition of subtle colouring to give the King the best possible impression of the castle and adjacent town to understand how they protected the harbour. As was the intention, the eye is drawn to the scale of Scarborough's defences. The castle is shown still in its late medieval grandeur with no sign of the decay of any of the walls or towers reported on by the two surveys of the previous year. A cannon shown in the middle of the headland pointing out to sea could be one of the weapons recorded as being stored in the castle keep at the time

of the 1538 survey by Sir Ralph Ellerker and Sir Marmaduke Constable.

The town defences are less impressive. The wall added at the end of the 15th century on the landward side of the town is clearly incomplete, with only a ditch and earth rampart in the central part. Another cannon is shown at the end of the pier guarding the entrance to the harbour, while, on the edge of the bay opposite, the artist shows a small round tower with battlements that looks like a form of gun emplacement current at the time. The pier may have originated in the 14th century but there is no evidence that either the gun position on the pier or the crenellated tower facing it ever existed and it may be that the view, like many of the others created for the King at this time, had a second purpose to show what the surveyor thought could be done to increase the defences of the port. The truth of the matter was that the castle was no longer adequate to provide an effective defence. Cannon first appeared on ships in the early 14th century and by the turn of the 16th century they were used in large numbers on warships. Although they lacked the destructive force and accuracy to sink enemy vessels easily, the cannon of the period were capable of disabling a ship by blowing away the rigging and killing and wounding the crew. A port like Scarborough, which was wide open to the sea, was vulnerable to attack by gunfire from ships anchored in the bay and, as Henry would now have appreciated, the castle, removed from the harbour and lacking fixed artillery positions, was too remote to deter a seaborne attack. This was starkly demonstrated during the Anglo-Scottish war of 1542-6 during the closing years of Henry's reign. In October 1544 three Scottish warships entered Scarborough bay and, within sight of the town and castle, proceeded to block the passage of merchant vessels sailing along the coast. With no artillery capable of firing out to sea, the castle garrison had no means of forcing the ships to leave the bay.

The castle was propelled on to the national stage again during the reign of Queen Mary when in April 1557 Sir Thomas Stafford, a nobleman with French sympathies and a force of 30 men, surprised the garrison and captured the castle as an act of defiance against the English Crown. However, he only held the castle for three days until forced to surrender to the much larger force of the earl of Westmorland. The incident lived on in folk memory and gave rise to the first printed work on Scarborough, called A brief ballad touching the traitorous seizure of Scarborough castle, published in London in 1577.

If the surveyor who compiled the sketch plan of Scarborough in 1539 was indeed in the town in March then he was here at exactly the same time as the King's commissioners charged with dissolving the town's three friaries. On 9 and 10 March the Franciscan, Dominican and Carmelite friaries, which had been a major part of the town's religious life for over two centuries, were assessed for their monetary value and then wound up. The Dominican friary was worth 15s. 4d., the Carmelite friary 10s. and the Franciscan friary was valued the least at 5s. 4d., perhaps in part reflecting the low value of the marshy ground it occupied at the centre of the medieval Old Borough. The comparatively low sums achieved tend to suggest that the friaries, like the rest of the town, had long since passed the peak of their medieval prosperity but their sudden passing must have been a tremendous shock to the ordinary people of Scarborough whose religious beliefs were rooted in tradition and the routine of religious observance.

The grounds of the friaries were quickly cleared of buildings and the stone and timber sold on for a profit. Soon afterwards the same fate befell the chapel of the Holy Sepulchre in St Sepulchre Street, which had stood since the 12th century but in the 1550s was left to fall into decay after the roof was stripped of lead and sold to pay for repairs to the pier. Much of the stone from the friaries and the chapel must also have found its way down to the harbour to be used on patching up the waterfront and pier. This probably explains why, at the turn of the 19th century, a magnificent medieval tombstone bearing the carving of a cross-legged knight at arms was discovered in the cellar of a shop near the pier. The stone was rescued and taken to the town hall and is now in the care of Scarborough Museum's Trust, though no-one knows who the figure is meant to represent. The tombstone was probably included in a load of stones from one of the demolished friary churches or the chapel of the Holy Sepulchre that had been taken for harbour repairs and then discarded for reuse as unsuitable because of the deeply incised carving or perhaps because of lingering religious sensitivity. The so-called Butter Cross, which stands at the top of West Sandgate and marks the site of one of the town's

37   The tombstone of an armed knight found in the cellar of a shop in the early 19th century.

38   The Butter Cross photographed at the beginning of the 20th century.

markets, also looks like it is reused from a medieval church. The origin of the stone is a mystery and is presumably not the original Butter Cross mentioned in medieval documents. Despite its traditional name it bears little resemblance to an actual cross. It stands about six feet high and though now badly weathered, early engravings of the cross show that it was decorated with panels and foliated leaves and resembles more the pinnacle found on a late medieval church than an actual cross. The Butter Cross stands barely a stone's throw from the site of the chapel of the Holy Sepulchre and the Franciscan friary and it is possible that it came from one of these buildings, perhaps deliberately retained and reused by the townsfolk to preserve a memory of the passing of these old religious establishments.

39 *Sketch plan of Scarborough town, castle and harbour compiled at the end of the 16th century.*

The Corporation faced a continuous struggle to maintain the harbour as a strong and safe anchorage throughout the 16th century. The Tudor traveller John Leland, who visited Scarborough around 1544, found 'the peere whereby socour is made for shippes is now sore decayeid, and that almost yn the middle of it'. The town requested money from Henry VIII to effect repairs and an Act of Parliament was passed in 1546 imposing a duty on vessels for repairing the pier, but this had little impact. The town had to wait another 20 years until the reign of Elizabeth I before any substantial sums were granted by the treasury to pay for the harbour repairs. In 1565 the Queen granted the sum of £500 along with 100 tons of timber and

six tons of iron to begin a wholesale rebuilding of the pier. The grant stipulated that the new pier had to be built wider and taller than its predecessor to provide greater protection for shipping and more resistance to storms and, though exact details of the construction are lost, a century later it was deemed one of the wonders of the town. In 1660 Dr Robert Wittie was sufficiently impressed by the scale of the Elizabethan pier to write:

Another [rarity] observable in this town is the mighty piers of stone, which are made of round stones many of them of some tons weight, which being laid loose [ie not cemented together] are yet piled together in such comely order, that stretching from the foot of the castle hill into

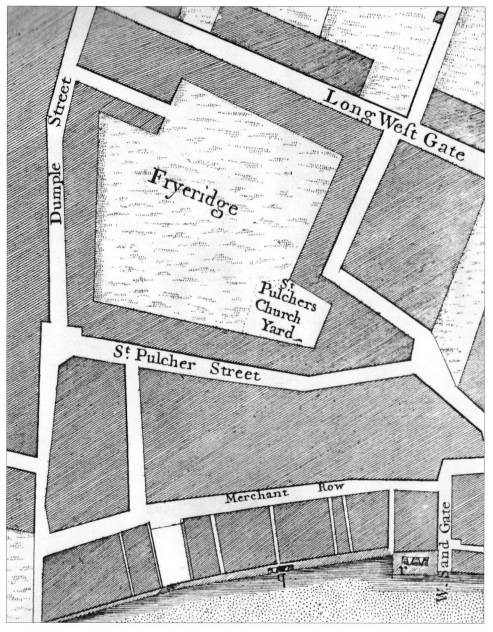

40 *The site of the Franciscan friary was still open ground at the time of Vincent's map of Scarborough, published in 1747.*

the sea they become a sure defence against the raging waves of the sea and make a convenient harbour for ships.

The picture that emerges of Scarborough in the 16th century is of a town in slow decline.

The castle no longer had any role as a strong defence, but lived on purely as a monument to the past, its wall ravaged by centuries of neglect. The unfinished town wall symbolised the loss of royal favour while the disappearance of the friaries and the chapel of the Holy Sepulchre

41 *A single-roomed building and cobbled street found in the north of Scarborough in 1988-9 was abandoned, along with large parts of the town, in the 16th century.*

signalled a strong break with the town's medieval past and presaged an uncertain future. The sites of the chapel and the friaries were not redeveloped but remained as scars on the town landscape, undoubtedly adding to the feeling of decline in the minds of the inhabitants. The town managed barely to survive on the twin staples of fishing and trade. The herring shoals still provided the town's fishing fleet with much profit in the late summer months but the port struggled to attract trade in the face of increasing competition from Hull, which was far better placed thanks to the network of navigable rivers that fed the River Humber to take advantage of the growing trade in textiles, coal and iron from the West Riding. So bad were the prospects for the town's markets that Scarborough went to

court to petition for the abolition of Seamer market when it was revived by Sir Henry Gate around 1576. When the inhabitants of Seamer stated that their market was better stocked and that the road to Scarborough was 'miry and evil' in the winter, Scarborough market seemed in danger of extinction. Even though the issue finally went in the town's favour with the final suppression of Seamer market in 1612, renewed prosperity was still a long way in the future. In 1605 a petition from the Corporation to James I, the first of the Stuart kings, asking for further money for the repair of the harbour, stated that 600 tenements in the town lay empty, which, if true, would have meant that large parts of Scarborough would have resembled a ghost town with derelict buildings lining deserted streets.

FOUR

Scarborough in the 17th Century

By the middle of the 17th century there were clear signs that the fortunes of the town were changing and Scarborough's economy was on the road to recovery. Locally, the most significant factor was the final suppression of the market at Seamer in 1612. If it had been allowed to continue unhindered the impact on Scarborough would have been disastrous as traders left the town, resulting in more deserted streets and boarded-up buildings. Scarborough's population could have shrunk to the size of a small fishing village. But this never happened. Securing the future of Scarborough's markets occurred just as agricultural productivity in the region was beginning to rise, which meant rising profits for the town's traders. In the same period, but on a much wider scale, the East Coast in the early 1600s saw a dramatic rise in the export of coal from the Durham and Northumberland coalfields through the ports of Newcastle and Sunderland to London and the continent. Scarborough benefited from the coal trade in two ways. Firstly, it provided vessels and crews to transport the coal, much of which was re-exported through Scarborough to the capital and across the North Sea to continental Europe and secondly it received the grant from parliament of the right to levy a fee on all coal moved down

the coast to help pay for the maintenance of the harbour. This came about after a violent storm in November 1613 wrecked the pier and rendered the harbour useless as a safe refuge for shipping plying the coastal routes. A petition from nearly all the ports from Newcastle down the East Coast to London that had vessels that used Scarborough harbour arrived at parliament soon after. It demanded that the government took action to help repair the harbour and secure it for the future as the only safe anchorage between the Humber and the Tyne. The following year, 1614, parliament imposed a levy on ships that used Scarborough amounting to 4d. on each ship under 50 tons and 8d. on each ship over that weight.

Suddenly the Corporation was awash with money for the harbour, allowing them to extend the Elizabethan pier further out into the bay and to strengthen the more exposed northern side by adding additional boulders. The income from the levy secured the future of the harbour, on which the fortunes of the town rested, and later the same century the coal trade provided an impetus to the town's shipbuilding industry through the construction of collier vessels. The industry was concentrated towards the eastern end of the harbour from approximately the position of King Richard III House to the foot of the castle headland. The Cockerill and Tindall families were instrumental in developing shipbuilding in Scarborough in the 1670s and 1680s, with the Tindalls maintaining a boat-building yard at Scarborough until 1863.

The Discovery of the Mineral Spring

An event that would have seemed quite minor at the time in 1626 was to have a profound and lasting influence on the future development of the town. That was the discovery of the mineral water spring on the shore of the South Bay. The person credited with the discovery by later authors was a Scarborough lady called Thomasin Farrer, the wife of John Farrer, one of the town's leading citizens. She noticed that rocks at the foot of the cliff about a quarter of a mile from the town were stained a red-brown colour by a spring issuing from the foot of the cliff. She discovered that the water from the spring had a distinct iron taste and found by drinking it that it had medicinal properties. At this date the only medicinal springs advertised in Yorkshire were the clusters of wells in the Forest of Knaresborough at modern-day Harrogate, whose health-giving reputation was probably known to a lady of Mistress Farrow's standing and helped her identify the spring at Scarborough for what it was. Situated on the sands and periodically covered by the high tides, the spring was open to anyone to try and Mistress Farrow was not able to profit from her discovery in the same way as if the spring had been on her husband's own land. As no-one had direct ownership of the spring to make a profit from it, there was no concerted effort to publicise the discovery. The reputation of the health-giving properties of the mineral spring at first spread only slowly, first among the inhabitants of Scarborough and then by word of mouth among the local nobility, to whom it came as an alternative to the Harrogate springs. A notable event in building the reputation of

the spa came at the end of the prolonged first siege of the castle in 1645 during the English Civil War. The royalist garrison of the castle, led by Sir Hugh Cholmley, was in bad health by the time the siege ended, with many suffering from scurvy, but are said to have been restored to health by the efficacy of the Scarborough spa waters. The Scarborough Historical Pageant performed in 1912 had Mistress Farrow in person leading the garrison to the spring with the words 'come then to founts of health I lead the way. all ye who ail and sicken follow I pray'. The same incident, without the involvement of Mistress Farrow, is described in Dr Robert Wittie's book on the Scarborough spa waters published in 1660. He writes, seemingly as an eyewitness to the events:

> The garrison that was kept by Sir Hugh Cholmley on the top of the castle hill, after a few weeks siege, whither from the air of the sea, or a bad diet, or want of exercise, were most of them taken to the scurvy, especially the country gentlemen, who had fled in thither, who were miserably troubled with it, as many of them drank of the spaw waters were perfectly and speedily cured, which some of them used without any other means.

The real growth in the popularity of the mineral spring at Scarborough did not start until the 1660s with the publication of Dr Wittie's book and the rash of others that followed advertising the existence of the spring and comparing the properties both favourably and unfavourably with the springs at Harrogate and elsewhere.

A good indication of Scarborough's recovery after 1600 is that the population began to rise for the first time since the Middle Ages. Detailed analysis of the baptism records from the parish church indicates that the population probably grew from the very low level of around 1,700 in 1600 to a much healthier figure of around 2,800 by 1640. This was despite the fact that Scarborough was visited during this period by the plague on at least three occasions necessitating the construction by the Corporation in 1626 of a 'pest house' in an isolated spot on the north side of the castle headland in the holms.

The Civil War

The start of the English Civil War was a major setback to the improving fortunes of the town. In 1642 the country was plunged in to several years of war that ended with the execution of King Charles I in January 1649 and the overthrow of the monarchy by parliament. For most of this tumultuous period Scarborough was on the periphery of the conflict but the town saw heavy fighting in 1645 and again in 1648 as parliamentary and royalist forces fought over control of the town and castle. The English Civil War is perhaps the most dramatic period in the long history of the town and it still casts a shadow as Scarborough to this day bears some of the physical scars of the fighting.

In the first months of the civil war Scarborough was held for parliament by Sir Hugh Cholmley of Whitby, one of the town's two MPs, with a garrison of several hundred men drawn from the town and local villages including his own Whitby estates. Sir Hugh readied the town and castle defences and mounted cavalry raids against royalist targets across the eastern part of Yorkshire almost to the walls of York, which was loyal to the king. But as the months passed Sir Hugh began to have doubts about the justness of the parliamentary cause and, in March 1643, he decided to change sides after a secret meeting with the Queen at York. Sir Hugh's decision to defect, which was supported by the majority of his forces in Scarborough, meant the likelihood of an attack on Scarborough subsided. With the royalists in the ascendant in the North of England there was no serious prospect of the parliamentarians mounting an attack to try and recapture Scarborough. But this all changed the following year with the

42 *Thomasin Farrer, as portrayed by Mrs Bevan in the Scarborough pageant of 1912.*

disastrous defeat of the royalist army in the North at the Battle of Marston Moor in July 1644, followed soon after by the surrender of York. Suddenly the military situation had changed and Scarborough very quickly became an isolated royalist outpost in a county that was now largely under the control of parliament. As long as Sir Hugh Cholmley remained loyal to the King an attack on Scarborough was inevitable as parliament could not afford to leave such an important port in royalist hands through fear of it being used to land reinforcements from the continent.

Sir Hugh did the best he could to prepare the castle for the anticipated attack. An artillery position was established on high ground forward of the main gate to command the approach to the castle along what is now Castle Road. It acquired the name of Bushell's Battery after one of Sir Hugh's officers. At the opposite end

of the headland on a platform of high ground overlooking the harbour, Sir Hugh created a second gun emplacement called the South Steel Battery. This was in a very vulnerable location at the foot of the headland well beyond the castle, to which it was linked by steps leading up the side of the castle dykes to a small gate in the curtain wall. This battery was so well sited to command the harbour that it was strengthened after the civil war and continued in use as a gun emplacement until the end of the 19th century. Along the foot of the castle dykes and in the castle holms on the north side of the headland

43 *The main entrance into the town at Newborough Bar was provided with new gates before the siege of Scarborough in 1645. Engraving by Francis Nicholson published in the 1820s.*

there are possible traces surviving of more ephemeral earthwork gun and infantry positions from this time, also constructed forward of the main castle defences. Within the castle, Sir Hugh ordered the medieval towers along the curtain wall to be reduced in height and their interiors filled with earth and rubble to create gun platforms looking out over the town. He knew that he stood very little chance of being able to defend the town itself and that its dilapidated medieval defences would not prove too much of an obstacle to bombardment and a determined assault by parliament.

This proved to be the case. The siege of Scarborough began in late January 1645 when the parliamentary commander, Sir John Meldrum, appeared at Falsgrave with a force of 1,200 English and Scottish soldiers. They attacked the town on 18 February and quickly broke through the defences, forcing the royalists to retreat back towards the safety of the castle. One of Sir Hugh Cholmley's officers, Sir Jordan Crosland, fought a brave rearguard action around the parish church to buy enough time for his leader and the rest of the garrison to make good their retreat into the castle. Sir John Meldrum

44   *The towers along the castle curtain wall dominate the town and were turned into artillery positions during the 1645 siege. Engraving published by Nathanial and Samuel Buck in 1745.*

may have captured the town on 18 February but he had missed his first and best chance to seize the castle. Instead he now faced a prolonged siege that cost many lives on both sides and finished at the end of July only when the castle garrison were too reduced by illness and starvation to continue to resist.

The course of the siege can be followed through Sir Hugh Cholmley's own memoirs and the accounts published in royalist and parliamentary news sheets. The South Steel Battery overlooking the harbour was captured as part of the initial assault on the town on 18 February while Bushell's Battery and the gatehouse area was at the heart of the fighting during much of the siege as Sir John Meldrum made repeated attempts to force his way into the castle. The siege took a new direction around the start of May when large artillery pieces arrived from York, including the most powerful cannon at parliament's disposal, capable of firing a ball weighing 65 pounds. This was positioned as close to the castle as possible within the chancel of the parish church, from where it fired repeatedly through the great east window at the keep. After three days of constant bombardment the keep, which had stood for nearly five hundred years, split in two and the west side collapsed in an avalanche of stone, choking the route into the castle from the gatehouse with rubble. The collapse of the keep was followed by a furious assault by the besieging forces, which the garrison repulsed by hurling the fallen stones down onto the attackers. There now followed

45 *The South Steel Battery overlooking the harbour was established as an artillery position by Sir Hugh Cholmley before the 1645 siege.*

46 *The area around the castle barbican and gatehouse was the scene of the bitterest fighting. In this watercolour drawing from the early 1800s, the earthwork embrassures of the royalist gun positions called Bushell's Battery can be seen in front of the barbican.*

47   *A Victorian photograph looking from the site of Bushell's Battery towards the parish church. The battery dominated the route up to the castle.*

the bloodiest part of the siege as both sides launched attack and counterattack for control of the gatehouse area. Sir John Meldrum was killed during this phase of the fighting and his replacement, Sir Matthew Boynton, decided to adopt a more cautious approach to the siege, relying on bombardment and starvation to achieve the surrender rather than direct hand-to-hand fighting. The siege dragged on for a few more months until, on 25 July, Sir Hugh Cholmley surrendered to stop the suffering of the garrison, many of whom had to be carried out of the castle in blankets. The defenders were given leave to join the nearest royalist garrison which was at Newark, but Sir Hugh Cholmley decided instead to go into exile.

Evidence of the 1645 siege still exists. The ragged profile of the castle keep bears witness to the sudden collapse of the west side during the bombardment of May 1645, while all that are left of the chancel of the parish church are two stumps of masonry marking the position of the east window, from where the devastating cannon fire was directed at the castle. The collapse of the rest of the chancel was brought about more by the heavy vibrations from the parliamentary cannon than the return fire from the castle, and later stone-robbing removed much of what had survived.

The castle was left under the command of Sir Matthew Boynton's son, also called Matthew, and by the spring of 1646 it is reported that work

48 *Half of the keep collapsed under bombardment during the 1645 siege and was never rebuilt.*

was under way to repair the castle defences and gatehouse. It is not recorded how much physical damage occurred in the town during the siege and how many casualties there were among the civilian population. Tradition has it that all the town's markets were suspended during the siege and were relocated to Peasholm, a mile to the north, where they were held under the watchful eye of a star-shaped parliamentary artillery emplacement guarding the North Bay. The fort survived as an earthwork until the 20th century and appears on early maps of the area as Oliver's Battery through some mistaken association with Oliver Cromwell.

The town had barely started to recover when conflict returned to Scarborough with the outbreak of the second English Civil War at the end of April 1648. Like Sir Hugh Cholmley before him, in July 1648 Sir Matthew Boynton, at first loyal to parliament, decided to change sides and join the royalist cause. Parliament, fearful of another prolonged and costly siege, tried persuasion, bribery and a blockade of the port to get him to reconsider. When these failed, a parliamentary force was dispatched to Scarborough from Hull at the end of July under the command of Colonel Bethell. Skirmishes took place around the outskirts of the town but the parliamentary force was too weak to mount a direct assault until September, when once again the royalists took refuge in the castle. Colonel Bethell seems not to have contemplated trying to mount any serious assaults on the castle but instead played a waiting game in the knowledge that the elsewhere in the country the renewed struggle was going parliament's way. The castle eventually surrendered in December, King Charles was executed at Whitehall the next month and Scarborough's experience of civil war came to an end. Although the 1648 siege was not as strongly or bloodily fought as in 1645 it did inflict more misery on a town that had already had more than its fair share of suffering and delayed the time when life in Scarborough would return to normal.

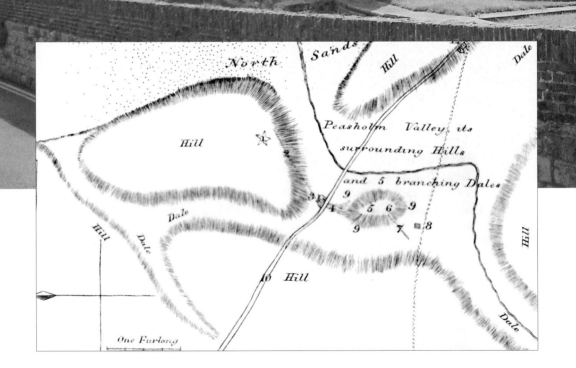

49 *The stumps of masonry from the medieval chancel destroyed in the 1645 siege.*

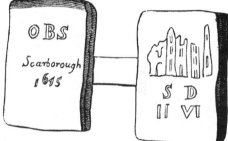

51   *Sir Hugh Cholmley issued his own coins during the siege to pay the garrison.*

50 left   *A sketch map of Peasholm, surveyed by Robert Knox in the 1850s, includes the site of the star-shaped civil war fort overlooking the north sands – labelled as 1 on the plan.*

Pyrologia Mimica,

OR, AN

ANSWER

TO

HYDROLOGIA CHYMICA

of WILLIAM SYMPSON

Phylo-Chymico-Medicus;

In DEFENCE of

SCARBROUGH-SPAW.

WHEREIN

The Five Mineral Principles of the said *Spaw* are defended against all his Objections by plain Reason and Experiments, and further confirmed by a Discovery of Mr. *S.* his frequent Contradictions and manifest Recantation.

ALSO

A Vindication of the Rational Method and Practice of Physick called *Galenical*, and a Reconciliation betwixt that and the *Chymical.*

Likewise a further Discourse about the ORIGINAL of SPRINGS.

By *ROBERT WITTIE*

Doctor in Physick.

LONDON,

Printed by *T. N.* for *J. Martyn* Printer to the *R. Society*, at the Bell without *Temple-Bar*, 1669.

52 *The title page of Robert Wittie's* Pyrologia Mimica, *one of 10 books published on the spa between 1660 and 1679.*

FIVE

The Early Spa

In the hundred or so years that followed the end of the English Civil War it is no exaggeration to claim that Scarborough invented the seaside holiday. By the 1740s the well-to-do from across the North of England and sometimes further afield were making regular visits in large numbers to Scarborough in the summer months to take the mineral waters discovered by Thomasin Farrer and enjoy other diversions including bathing in the sea and banqueting, gambling and dancing in the evenings at the town's assembly rooms. At first the popularity of Scarborough spa was slow to build. The end of the civil war followed by the period of Cromwell's protectorate was hardly the right time for the landed gentry to contemplate gathering in large numbers at the seaside but the restoration of the monarchy in 1660 marked a return to freer times.

The same year also saw the appearance in print of the first in a remarkable series of books published between 1660 and 1679 in which Doctors Wittie, Simpson and Tonstall each put forward their own analyses of the mineral contents and curative properties of the spa waters. Although the authors were participating in a serious scientific and medical debate these books, published variously in York and London, brought the existence of Scarborough spa to

the attention of a wide readership among the gentry. Among all the verbiage surrounding the mineral properties of the spa waters, the books are invaluable in the short glimpses they give of the early spa and its visitors. Doctor Wittie described the appearance of the mineral spring in 1660 as like a boiling pot on the beach as the water bubbled out of the ground producing some 24 gallons of water in an hour. He recommended the patient should start at the spa by drinking two half-pints of the water, preferably before seven a.m. and at the spring itself, which entailed an early morning walk or carriage drive along the beach from the town. He did admit, though, that those who were too infirm to make the journey could partake of the water in their chambers. After drinking the specified dose, the patient was recommended to walk along the beach for at least half an hour. As time wore on visitors were told to increase the amount they drank while still trying to complete the dose before 10 in the morning. Dr Wittie suggested the patient should stay in Scarborough for around a month to five weeks to gain the benefit of drinking the water and that they should try and make their visit between mid-May and mid-September to take advantage of the summer months. This was not surprising as, at the time Dr Wittie was writing, there was no shelter at the spa and the visitors presumably had to drink the water either standing or sitting on the beach while exposed to the elements. However, through these recommendations Dr Wittie had created the idea of a summer season at Scarborough. It was many decades before accommodation purpose-built for summer visitors began to appear. Visiting the spa in 1665 and 1666 with his wife, Henry Newcome recorded that he had tried to stay at an inn but, that being full, he was forced to rent rooms in a private house. This must have been most visitors' experience throughout the 17th century as in 1686 the war office returns found there were only 74 guest beds available in the town, hardly sufficient to accommodate the number of visitors that even then the spa was attracting each summer.

Dr Wittie noted that visitors went to the spa for pleasure and to withdraw themselves for a while from their serious employment, while Dr Simpson, writing in 1679, observed that some visitors came chiefly for the diversions and only played with the water. These two statements document the beginning of the idea that a stay at the seaside could be as much about finding pleasure as finding health and so mark the birth of the seaside holiday. Some idea of the widening knowledge of the spa can be gained from the medical histories contained in some of the early spa water books. In his second book on the spa, published in 1667, Dr Wittie's Historical Relation of the Cures mentions patients from the city of York and other parts of the county and from Manchester, Northrop and Grimsby in Lincolnshire, Bolam and Berwick-upon-Tweed in Northumberland and even an individual from London. Dr Simpson's 1679

book The History of Scarborough Spaw gives a comparable geographical spread of patients including two ladies from Scotland cured of scurvy and the stone.

The Corporation owned the spa because of its situation on the beach and they began levying a small charge for drinking the water in 1684.

53 *A view of Scarborough published by Thomas Gent in 1734.*

In 1699 they ordered the construction of a cistern and pipes at the foot of the cliff to collect the spring water so that they could better regulate consumption and apply the charges. In a magnanimous gesture, the local poor were allowed to drink the water for free. A few years later several buildings had appeared at the cistern and are shown on the first view of the spa drawn by Francis Place sometime around 1715 and published in 1731. The view shows a house for the ladies, a house for gentlemen to retire in and 'Dickie's house' sharing a terrace at the foot of the cliff. The latter is a reference to Richard Dickinson, the first recorded governor

54 *Richard Dickinson, the first governor of Scarborough spa.*

55 *A Victorian engraving depicting Richard Dickinson at the spa in the 1730s.*

of Scarborough spa, who was widely regarded for his wit and ready humour despite being, as one contemporary described him, 'one of the most deformed pieces of mortality I ever saw, and of most uncouth manner of speech'.

Then as now effective marketing was the key to a prosperous resort, and so the medical treatises of learned doctors from the 17th century were joined in the 18th century by literature of a more palatable kind. The anonymous description of the town published by the London booksellers Ward and Chandler in 1734 entitled A Journey from London to Scarborough in Several Letters from a Gentleman there leaves no doubt this is a place worth visiting. Gone are the exhaustive analyses of the spa waters, replaced by a beguiling and entertaining picture of the town's varied attractions, including two miles of sand as level as a bowling green, reasonably priced and well-furnished accommodation, wide streets for coaches to pass, and the company of the nobility. Two dukes, seven earls, one marquis, 19 baronets and six knights signed the subscription books at the spa, the long room, the booksellers' shop

and the coffee house. Scarborough was firmly established as the Northern seaside equivalent of fashionable Epsom, Bath or Tunbridge. There were also attractive engravings of the town to entice the prospective visitor. Without exception these showed the town from across the South Bay, giving due prominence to the now-famous spa and the bowling-green sands. Among the more detailed of the 18th-century views of Scarborough was that published by John Setterington in 1735. Fashionably attired men and women are shown at leisure rowing small boats around the bay, or galloping horses on the beach and plunging about in the waves, while the more timorous swim from a small wooden hut on wheels half submerged in the water, the first depiction of the seaside bathing machine that was to be a familiar sight at Scarborough and other seaside resorts until the early 20th century. Swimming in the sea at Scarborough was first recommended as a cure for gout by Dr Wittie in the 1667 edition of his book on the spa. By the 1730s it was a common pastime indulged in for pleasure and for health: 'It is the custom for not only the Gentlemen, but the Ladies also, to bath in the Sea: The Gentlemen go out a little way to sea in Boats (called here Cobbles) and jump in naked directly … the Ladies have the Convenience of Gowns and Guides.'

Of course, not everyone agreed that Scarborough was the seat of mirth or found the town quite as salubrious as depicted in the engravings. One visitor in 1741 thought the daily routine of dining, dancing and drinking the spa water was farcical and over-priced, complaining that Scarborough was as costly as London. More specific in her criticism was Sarah, Duchess of Marlborough, who spent six weeks in Scarborough in July and August 1732 to take the spa waters. The widow of the great general the Duke of Marlborough and familiar with the comforts of Blenheim Palace, she seemed to take an immediate dislike to Scarborough. With no tourism department to complain to, letters to friends contained her ill feelings towards the town and its spa. She claimed her accommodation was very bad, very dirty and very noisy from the horses and coaches passing her window. Of the company she wrote, 'one would not choose rather to be deaf and dumb than to be with them', and as for the spa being the equal of Tunbridge or Epsom she found it 'very dirty and expresses vast poverty in every part of it. It is besides so extremely steep and disagreeable to get to either in a coach or chair, that I resolve to go no more, but to take my waters at home.' She was certainly right to complain about the poor access to the spa, which could only be reached either by a long trek along the beach at low tide or by a tortuous footpath down the cliff from modern St Nicholas Cliff.

The Duchess's demand for better company might have been fulfilled if royalty had favoured Scarborough. The sight of a prince or princess bathing in the South Bay would have attracted more nobility to Scarborough than all the

guidebooks and engravings put together, but sadly it was never to be though not for lack of trying. Her Royal Highness the Princess Amelia received an invitation to visit in the form of a poem published in 1734. The town, the poet told her, was only surpassed by ancient Baiae, the resort of imperial Rome, but, were she 'to visit Scarborough's springs and breath its air, the lustre borrowed from her greater name, would Scarborough raise above old Baiae's fame'. The reaction of the Princess Amelia to this impassioned plea is not recorded.

The distance from London posed a problem for anyone travelling from the capital to Scarborough, but it was not an insurmountable one. Scarborough could be reached in three or four days by boat from London, and for the ordinary traveller the usual procedure was to barter for passage on one of the colliery vessels sailing out of Billingsgate that voyaged up the coast to Newcastle. Overland journeys by stagecoach took longer than the boat and were more expensive, and probably left the traveller just as queasy as a rough sea journey.

Scarborough's development as a spa town nearly came to an abrupt end on 29 December 1737 when, with a loud crack, the cliff behind gave way and over quarter of a million tons of clay and earth slipped forwards onto the beach. Thankfully no one was injured and even the cattle continued to graze as the pasture they were feeding on slipped slowly down the cliff. There had been several warning rumbles of the impending landslip the previous day, but there was nothing that could be done to prevent what happened and the spa waters stopped flowing. Scarborough Corporation was mortified. By 1737 there were two cisterns side by side, the second receiving water of a slightly different composition to the first, though it required a sensitive palate to distinguish between them. The purgative spring furthest from the town was distinctly bitterish, the chalybeate 'more brisk, quick or pungent'. The second spring had been a very timely discovery, doubling the capacity of the spa around the time the first facilities were provided for the comfort of those drinking the waters. The landslip swept all this away. Richard Dickinson, the governor of the spa, lost both his house with its well-stocked wine cellar and his livelihood with the loss of the spa cisterns. The shock proved too much for poor Richard Dickinson and he died six weeks later, leaving the Corporation to sort out the mess.

It soon became clear what had happened. About an acre of land had split away from the cliff and slid forwards onto the beach. This forced the comparatively soft beach sand forwards and upwards, collapsing the sea wall around the spa buildings before the whole lot, including the spa cisterns, was buried below the earth and clay brought down by the cliff slip. Called by some contemporaries 'The Scarborough Earthquake', this was only the latest in a series of disasters to have befallen the spa. Damage from heavy seas was a recurrent problem; only the previous year the Corporation had been forced to spend £20 commissioning an engineer to rebuild the sea wall totally following one bad storm. Minor cliff falls were a constant nuisance, damaging the buildings and almost killing one visitor, a Mr Hanbury, in 1732.

After the landslide some sceptics imagined the mineral springs were lost forever, but the Corporation appreciated the importance of the spa to Scarborough and acted decisively to restore them. They organised teams of workmen to dig away tons of earth and rubble from the spot where the cisterns had stood.

56   *The overland route to Scarborough depicted on Ogilby's route map published in the 1720s.*

57 *An enlargement of Thomas Gent's view of Scarborough published in 1734, showing the spa before the landslip.*

A contemporary engraving shows the work in progress. Carts waited in turn at the foot of the landslip to take the spoil further down the beach for dumping. Their efforts were rewarded and, on 16 February 1738, the corporation announced in the pages of the London Daily Post that the spring had been rediscovered, that it was appointing a new governor and that it planned to erect more commodious and better-protected buildings to receive visitors to the spa.

Scarborough had been lucky. The landslide had occurred during the winter when there was

58 *Engraving of the landslip made in 1738 showing cows still grazing on the block of cliff affected.*

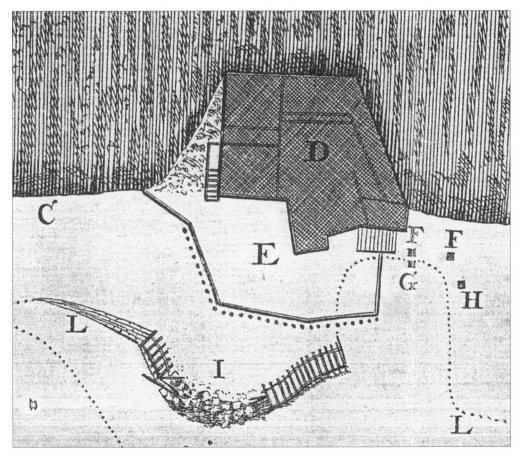

59 *Plan from 1738 of the landslip, showing the extent to which the staith protecting the spa buildings (labelled E) had been forced forwards onto the beach by the force of the slip (labelled I).*

60 *The top of the 1737 landslip today.*

little demand for the mineral springs and the speedy discovery of the waters meant the supply could be restored in good time for the next season. Not leaving anything to chance, the Corporation announced in the pages of the York Courant newspaper on 25 April 1738 that the spa was restored and capable of supplying any quantity of bottled water that gentlemen or dealers might require. In June the same paper carried an article by the eminent physician Dr Peter Shaw, who four years previously had published an exhaustive scientific analysis of the spa waters. He repeated his experiments, concluding that the waters purged just as strongly as before and had the same health-giving properties. When, on 25 August, the Courant reported on the distinguished company at the spa, drinking water of the greatest perfection, Scarborough's reputation had been saved. The new spa buildings were higher up the cliff and the two cisterns had been brought within the shelter of a new sea wall. The wall was a huge structure measuring five yards high and, like the harbour walls, was constructed of massive boulders interlaced with timbers. Their swift action in rebuilding the spa testifies to the fact that the Corporation clearly recognised the importance of the mineral spring to the town and the wealth and fame it had already brought to Scarborough. For the next 200 years the well-being of the spa was always high on the list of the Corporation's priorities.

Though Scarborough was the country's first seaside resort and, until King George III chose to dip his feet in the English Channel at Brighton in 1789, arguably its most fashionable, there was nothing particularly unique about the amenities and entertainments it offered the visitor. The social life of the well-to-do visitor and resident alike revolved around the spa, the assembly rooms, the theatre and the coffee shops and all, apart from the spa, could have been found in any prosperous Georgian market town. Hull opened its assembly rooms in 1752, Sheffield in 1762 and York in 1731-2, while all large towns possessed a theatre, Scarborough being part of the Northern circuit for professional touring companies who also stopped off at Richmond, Ripon, Whitby, Harrogate, Northallerton, Guisborough and Beverley.

61 *The spa as it was rebuilt after the 1737 landslip. Engraving by Francis Nicholson, published in the 1820s.*

62   *The spa was given massive sea defences after the 1737 landslip. Engraving by J. Stubbs, published in 1825.*

The town's first assembly or long room was on the seafront facing on to the harbour, hardly the most fashionable part of the town. In the 1720s new assembly rooms were opened at the southern end of present-day St Nicholas Street (which for a while afterwards was known as Long Room Street) on the present site of the *Royal Hotel.* Known as Donner's Assembly Rooms after the first proprietor, it was joined by a rival establishment in the same street in 1736, owned by Mr Newstead. During the day the tall windows of Donner's Assembly Rooms gave a magnificent view out to sea but, at night, illuminated like a court assembly, the venue really came alive. Balls were held each evening in the 1730s, the elegant dances accompanied from the gallery by the orchestra. At one end of the room games of chance were on offer, or alternatively cards in the side rooms and billiards downstairs until around 10 or 11 p.m. when the company started to drift back to their lodgings.

As an alternative to the company at the spa or the assembly rooms, the coffee house at the junction of present-day Newborough and St Thomas Street offered a fresh diversion and the chance to catch up on the London newspapers brought by ship from the capital. The town's only theatre stood a little way further on down St Thomas Street. Added to these attractions were a circulating library, bookshop, a selection of inns and shops selling all manner of goods from poultry to fish sauces. The Georgian visitor to Scarborough's more fashionable streets could have imagined themselves in any town in the country; businesses with a distinctive seaside character were still few and far between.

SIX

Georgian and Regency Scarborough

When, in 1745, Scarborough was forced to take measures to defend itself against a possible attack by the rebel army of Bonnie Prince Charlie, it was simply a question of resurrecting the town's medieval defences, since they still marked the limits of the built-up area some 500 years after they were constructed. The rising popularity of the spa and the influx of summer visitors had not yet had any significant impact on the size of the town or on the livelihood of its inhabitants. In 1745 and for decades afterwards shipbuilding and coastal trade were the mainstays of the town's economy. The first Scarborough guidebook, published in 1787, remarks upon 'the sound of industry on its strand' and claims that 'the visitors of distinction in pursuit of health, or the amusements of a gay throng, cannot turn their eyes any whither without being entertained by the delightful, busy and picturesque scene'. Most families in the town had some connection with the harbour and seamen made up a large percentage of the town's population. The 1786 muster roll records 665 seamen in Scarborough when the total population probably amounted to no more than six thousand. The fishing industry too was important but Thomas Hinderwell, writing towards the close of the century, stated

that he had witnessed a steady decline during the preceding three decades.

The threat posed by the Jacobite rebellion in 1745 was taken very seriously by the government, who feared the rebel army would attempt to capture an East Coast port in the North of England in order to land reinforcements from the continent. Some 900 barrels of gunpowder and arms for 36,000 men were stockpiled in the castle keep, while a commission for the defence of Scarborough was set up to organise the town's defences. By October 1745 the town had raised the sum of £300 by voluntary subscription to pay for new fortifications, which included recutting the old medieval ditch on the landward side of the town and building gun batteries to defend the harbour and the approaches from the west, deploying 99 cannon brought from the ships in the harbour. In the event, Scarborough was not directly threatened as Bonnie Prince Charlie led his army into England down the west side of the Pennines. After the invasion scare had passed, and perhaps with a slight tinge of anticlimax, the committee commissioned a plan of the fortifications to demonstrate the considerable efforts they had made to defend Scarborough while the government stepped in to make more

63 *The castle was garrisoned until very nearly the end of the 19th century. This engraving dates from the 1850s.*

lasting improvements to the castle defences. Sir Hugh Cholmley's South Steel Battery overlooking the harbour was totally rebuilt with room for 12 18-pounder guns to protect the seaward side of Scarborough. The battery was protected by thick stone walls reinforced by wide earthen banks to withstand enemy artillery, and a stone wall constructed up the side of the castle dykes called 'the covered way' provided a protected route for the gunners to and from the castle. A permanent garrison was established within the castle, accommodated in new barracks of red brick built halfway along the curtain wall overlooking the town on the site of the medieval Mosdale Hall. To secure an increased water supply for the garrison, an underground reservoir was built close to the cliff edge, within the footprint of the now-buried Roman signal station, to collect water from the spring there. The Master Gunner's House on

the north side of the headland, incorporating a magazine in the basement, also dates to this period, although recent analysis of the fabric suggests it may preserve elements of a building dating from the early 1700s. The changes to the castle in 1746 meant it was once again fit to be permanently garrisoned and it continued to house military units and artillery until very nearly the end of the 19th century.

The harbour began a new phase of development in the 1730s with plans to construct a new pier from the foot of the castle headland aligned to the seawards of the original pier, which was itself extended. As well as increasing the capacity of the port, the new pier was needed as a breakwater to provide additional protection to the harbour. An Act of Parliament passed in 1732 provided the funds by giving the town the income from charges levied on coal leaving Newcastle and its sister ports. The work proceeded slowly. Huge barges carried the stone for building work from quarries across the South Bay at the headland of White Nab where the work to crane the huge blocks onto the barges made an entertaining spectacle for visitors to the nearby spa. After more than 10 years of work Vincent's map of 1747 shows only a short stub of the new pier projecting out into the bay, and five years later a new Act of Parliament was passed to address issues over the misappropriation of some of the money. Work on the new pier continued right through the remainder of the 18th century and was not completed until 1826. One unforeseen problem was that the new pier seemed to exacerbate the problem of silting, which seriously reduced the depth of water in the harbour and threatened its long-term future. Gaps were created in both the old and new piers to try and get nature to wash the sand out of the harbour, but these

were only partially successful, necessitating the use of labourers to dig the sand out of the harbour at low tide.

One interesting proposal from the end of the 18th century to help develop the commerce of the port was to connect Scarborough to the canal network to improve communication and the movement of goods inland. The idea was put forward in 1769 by a local surgeon, John Travis, as a possible measure to arrest the decline in the town's fishing industry, which by that date only employed 105 men. A canal would open up a market for the town's fish among the rapidly expanding urban populations of the West Riding and across the Pennines to Manchester. The idea was put forward again at the end of the century and estimates prepared. The proposal was for the construction of over 23 miles of canal, with a width of 30ft and depth of 4.5ft, to connect the harbour at Scarborough to the Costa Beck

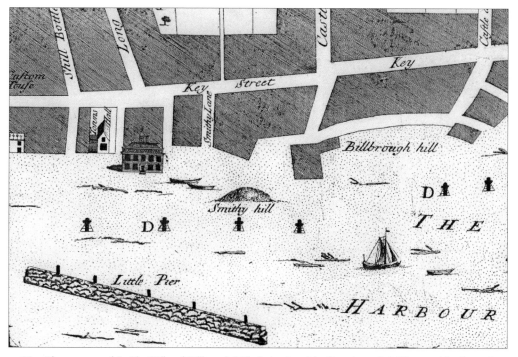

64 *The area around Smithy Hill and Billbrough Hill, depicted on John Setterington's 1725 map of Scarborough, was where the shipbuilding industry became established in the second half of the 17th century.*

65 *The outer pier photographed at the start of the 19th century. Work to build the outer pier began in the 1730s.*

66   *A crane lies idle on the new outer pier, depicted by Francis Nicholson in 1822.*

67   *The lighthouse was constructed on the end of Vincent's pier around 1807. Engraving by J. Stubbs, published in 1825.*

near Pickering and from there to construct a further branch to the River Derwent at Malton to gain access to the river systems and canal of the Vale of York and the Humber Basin. This ambitious scheme would have required the construction of a sea lock and canal basin at Scarborough, with another 24 locks along the line of the canal inland to Pickering. The canal would have become the principal artery for the movement of agricultural produce around the towns and villages of the Vale of Pickering and for the transport of goods inland from the port at Scarborough. Although the carefully calculated figures indicated an annual profit of 7.5 per cent by setting a toll of 3d. per ton per mile on the movement of goods, the scheme was never implemented and the town continued to have to rely on a road system of variable quality for all its communication inland until the coming of the railway in 1845.

It is unlikely that the well-to-do spa visitors ventured too far into the streets and alleyways of the old town to view the working life of the harbour at close range. One later writer declared these same streets in 1803 to be 'disagreeable beyond description' and ' a stranger to pure air'. The accommodation and amusements for the visitors were mostly in the more salubrious western half of the town, well away from the hustle and bustle of the harbour. In Newborough and the streets adjoining were to be found the theatre, the assembly rooms, the inns and the coffee house, while most of the visitors stayed in lodging houses along Queen Street and Merchant's Row.

The construction of a carriageway, now called Bland's Cliff, down onto the sands from Newborough in 1722 was the first major addition to the street pattern since the Middle Ages and an early indication that the rising importance of the spa was influencing the physical growth of the town. The road was constructed by John Bland,

68   The theatre in St Thomas Street was constructed in 1767, replacing an earlier establishment of the 1730s. This advertising poster is from 1830.

one of the town's Quaker merchants, as a more convenient route onto the beach primarily for those wanting access along the sands to the spa. The winding and steep route down the cliff side was paved along its entire length and protected by a timber staith at the bottom where it was exposed to the sea, for which Mr Bland received the sum of £85 from the Corporation. Buildings soon appeared along the length of the new road, one of which came to house the town's first printing press, opened by Thomas Gent of Hull in 1734.

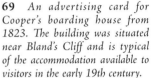

69 *An advertising card for Cooper's boarding house from 1823. The building was situated near Bland's Cliff and is typical of the accommodation available to visitors in the early 19th century.*

Scarborough's 'New Town'

The 1760s saw the start of the first sustained period of growth in the physical size of the town since the addition of the New Borough 600 years earlier in the reign of Henry II. Between the 1760s and the 1830s the steady addition of new buildings and streets across former agricultural land on the south-west of the town amounted to what some contemporaries described as Scarborough's 'New Town', although now the architectural integrity of this area is somewhat obscured by later developments and more recent demolitions. The impetus for this period of expansion was almost entirely driven by the continued growth in the popularity of the spa and the need to provide more attractive and salubrious accommodation than that on offer in the confines of the old town. Established wisdom held that the south-west side of a town was the healthiest and this too must have influenced the choice of the St Nicholas Cliff area for the first stage of the development. This saw the construction of a terrace of large

70　　*Taking the spa waters in 1812.*

71　　*Visitors enjoying the south sands in 1812.*

72 *St Nicholas Cliff in an engraving published by J. Stubbs in 1825.*

73 *A portion of the map of Scarborough published in 1811 in the second edition of Thomas Hinderwell's* History of Scarborough *shows the extent of development on 'The Cliff' and Dr Falconer's 'New Road'.*

74 *The houses of the 'New Town' are glimpsed beyond the trees in this view of Scarborough published by Francis Nicholson in 1822.*

houses for letting as lodgings for well-to-do visitors. The terrace was fronted by an oval carriageway and gardens that gave open 'picturesque' views across the sands to the spa. The new buildings were large enough to accommodate three or four families with their servants. From The Cliff, as it became known, there was a comparatively short, if steep, descent to the sands at a point barely 400 yards from the spa wells while The Cliff itself became popular with visitors as an evening promenade. The gentility of the location was from time to time interrupted by 'numerous groups of unwashed artificers', who took delight in annoying the gathered crowds by their boisterous behaviour and impolite language 'most offensive to the delicacy of our lovely country-women'.

From The Cliff, development proceeded gradually westwards over the following years as local speculators bought up blocks of land

75 *The upper-floor windows of the houses in Falconer's Square would have enjoyed views down the coast when built in the early 1800s.*

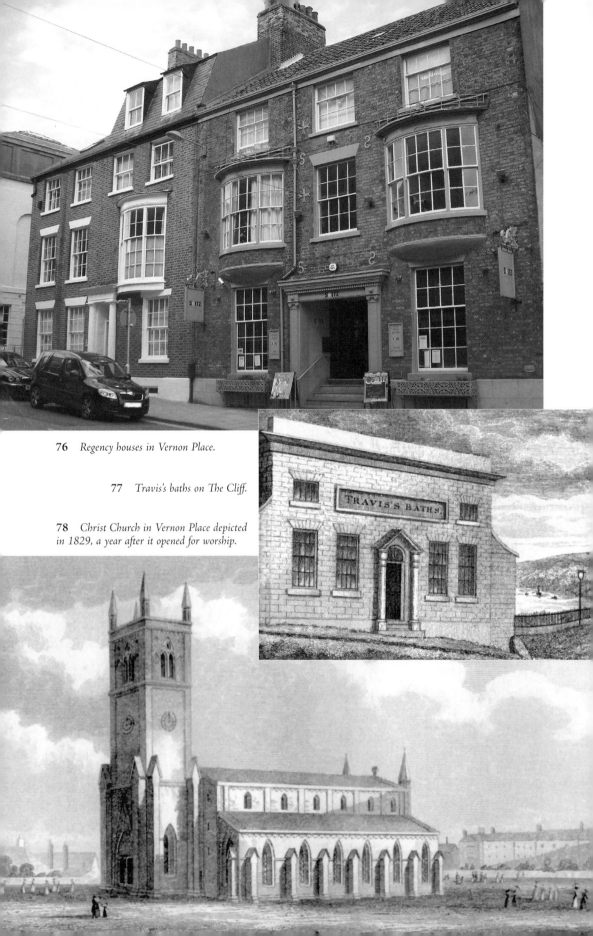

76 *Regency houses in Vernon Place.*

77 *Travis's baths on The Cliff.*

78 *Christ Church in Vernon Place depicted in 1829, a year after it opened for worship.*

for building. In 1779 Joseph Huntriss paid for the construction of a new road starting from the *Pied Bull Inn* outside Newborough Bar towards the spa, running parallel and outside the course of the town defences. By 1811 the first part of the road from the *Pied Bull Inn*, then called the *Bull Inn*, was lined with buildings and had become known as Huntriss Row. In 1792 a retired medical man from Lichfield called Dr Falconer paid for the construction of a new road heading westwards from St Nicholas Cliff and then southwards down into the valley to provide a more gentle descent from the town to the sands. It was opened as a toll road for visitors to the spa from which carts and wagons were excluded. Dr Falconer's new road opened up more ground for development and the following years saw the addition westwards from Huntriss Row of Falconer's Square, Vernon Place and Brunswick Terrace along the north side of the new road. The architecture of Scarborough's 'New Town' lacked the grandeur of contemporary developments at other spa towns. The varied building styles evident from 19th-century engravings and from the buildings that have survived testify to the small scale and piecemeal nature of the overall development.

Among the new lodging houses that bordered St Nicholas Cliff, Falconer's Road and the streets leading off it the visitor could also enjoy several specialist shops, such as those on The Cliff run by Mr Crawford and Mr Cracknell selling seashells of 'great variety and exquisite beauty', while ornaments of Derbyshire Spar, fossils and 'foreign birds of beautiful plumage' could be acquired from a shop in Huntriss Row. For those visitors too timorous to try bathing in the sea, the New Town offered several privately run seawater baths. The first to open in the town were Travis's Baths on The Cliff. They opened in 1798 and were substantially rebuilt in 1822 with interiors 'fitted up with every attention

to comfort and elegance' and supplied with the purest seawater at every tide. The demand for heated seawater baths grew and, by 1825, there were two other bathing establishments established in this part of the town – Harland's Baths on the corner of Falconer's Road and Vernon Place and Champley's Baths on the south side of Falconer's Road, midway between The Cliff and Brunswick Terrace. Both Travis and Harland were well-established doctors in Scarborough and Champley was a chemist with a shop on Newborough, associations that highlight the health-giving properties that were believed to attach to seawater bathing at this period.

The growth in size of the New Town led in the 1820s to demands that it should have its own place of worship to alleviate pressure in the summer from visitors attending the parish church. Public subscription raised £3,000 towards the cost of the new building, which, as Christ Church, opened for worship in August 1828 in Vernon Place. Designed by the York architect Peter Atkinson in the Gothic style of the 13th century it used a sandy limestone from the nearby village of Hackness, which proved to have poor resistance to weathering and the building eventually had to be demolished in 1979. In August 1829 the New Town acquired a second major building with the opening of the town's first public museum, the Rotunda, by the Scarborough Philosophical Society. The creation of the Scarborough Philosophical Society is an indication of the growing numbers of professional people living in Scarborough in the Regency period. Research has shown that the gentry and professional classes increased the most during the period from 1777 and 1823. This found expression in the 1820s with plans to found a philosophical society in the town to promote science and investigate the natural history of Scarborough and its region in imitation of the learned societies found in Leeds, York, Hull and Whitby. The philosophical society was formally constituted in April 1828 with the ambitious objective of founding a museum. The society immediately decided to erect its own building rather than go down the path of finding a building to rent and lighted upon a location close to the sands below St Nicholas Cliff that offered 'the greatest advantage of publicity and prospect'. They decided that a novel, circular design for the new museum was ideally suited to displaying the geology of the region and put the detailed planning in the hands of the York architect R.H. Sharp, whose building soon became known as the 'Rotunda'. The museum

opened at the end of August 1829, displaying geological and natural history specimens donated from several private collections including that of Thomas Hinderwell, the town's first historian, who had passed away four years previously. With a single admission ticket costing 1s. for an adult and 6d. for a child under 14, the museum at first appealed mainly to the better-off summer visitors. The Rotunda was extended in 1860 with the addition of two wings and since 2008 has been the William Smith Museum of Geology, named after the father of English geology who was employed as a land agent at Hackness at the time the Rotunda was being planned and was influenced its innovative design.

79 *The Rotunda Museum and Cliff Bridge depicted in 1829.*

80 *Wings were added to the Rotunda Museum in 1860.*

The crowning achievement of this phase of the town's development was the construction of the Cliff Bridge, which opened two years before the Rotunda Museum in July 1827. The intention in building the bridge was, for the first time, to provide visitors with an even and not too steep descent from the town to the spa that avoided the necessity of crossing the sands. The Scarborough Cliff Bridge Company was formed at a meeting in York in November 1826 and resolved that its object was to 'erect an Iron Bridge, supported by massy stone piers … to be thirteen feet wide, for foot passengers only' extending from the cliff across the valley to the Spa Cliff, from where it was proposed to construct a terrace down the cliff side to the spa. Investors came forward from the town to buy shares in the enterprise and an engineer, Mr John Outhett, was appointed at the end of November to design the bridge. Early the

following year Scarborough Corporation granted the company a 99-year lease on the spa itself, opening up the prospect that the monies raised from the tolls on the new bridge would lead to improvements at the spa. The bridge was opened in July 1827 with speeches and a procession of civic dignitaries, ending with the unexpected yet entertaining spectacle of a brave 'British Tar', who crossed the bridge standing upright on a galloping mail coach 'to the imminent danger of his own life and to the very great terror of the multitude of spectators'.

What could be read as the final phase in the development of the 'New Town' came between the mid-1830s and 1850s with the laying out of

81 *Thomas Hinderwell, Scarborough's first historian.*

82 *Before the construction of the Cliff Bridge visitors to the spa from the 'New Town' had to follow a tortuous route down the valley side from St Nicholas Cliff.*

83 *The Cliff Bridge and the terrace beyond leading to the spa, photographed at the beginning of the 20th century.*

84 *The Crescent, constructed between 1833 and 1857.*

85 *The tea garden at Scalby Mills at the north end of the North Bay sands was a favourite with visitors in the early 19th century.*

86 *The view from the Scalby Mills tea garden in an engraving published in the 1820s.*

87 *Survey of Scarborough by A.Tyson in 1842, three years before the coming of the railway.*

Belvoir Terrace and the Crescent on an elevated site overlooking Ramsdale Valley to the south-west of Brunswick Terrace. The development was completed by several large villa residences facing towards the crescent of terrace houses, two of which later in the century became the summer residences of Lord Londesborough and the famous literary family, the Sitwells.

SEVEN

Victorian Scarborough

The Coming of the Railway

The gradual development of Scarborough's 'New Town' in the late Georgian and Regency periods was easily eclipsed in scale by the expansion that occurred in the second half of the 19th century after the coming of the railway. From the early beginnings in 1834 with the opening of Yorkshire's first railway between Leeds and Selby, the 1840s saw a massive expansion of the rail network across the county including, in 1845, the opening of the line between York and Scarborough. It was built and operated by the York and North Midlands Railway under the chairmanship of the later disgraced 'Railway King' of York, George Hudson. As early as 1839 Hudson, along with his engineer George Stephenson, had been in the town to put forward the idea of building a railway line to Scarborough, which at that time was easily the most populous town on the Yorkshire coast with its port and holiday trade an obvious target for connection to the railway network. In a pamphlet published the following year George Knowles, a wealthy engineer who had retired to Scarborough and lived at Woodend, one of the large villa residences around the Crescent, questioned the desirability of linking Scarborough to the

burgeoning railway network. He feared that many of the 'respectable' visitors who came to Scarborough by stagecoach would desert the resort under the tide of vagrants brought by the railway. Looking to the future, Knowles thought that for Scarborough 'the novelty of not having a railroad will be its greatest recommendation', but his protests fell on deaf ears. A few months after the publication of Knowles's pamphlet the shareholders of the York and North Midlands Railway, meeting in July 1840, agreed a sum of up to £500 for a survey of the route to Scarborough and for a branch line to Pickering. Delays then ensued over objections to the proposed route out of York but work eventually began in July 1844, with Hudson setting himself the challenge that the line would be opened within a year. He succeeded. The opening ceremony was held on 7 July 1845 when an estimated crowd of between 10,000 and 15,000 people gathered at Scarborough to witness the arrival of the first train, pulled by the engines Hudson and Lion. The first passengers disembarked to find the terminus building at Scarborough still under construction with a temporary roof formed from awnings.

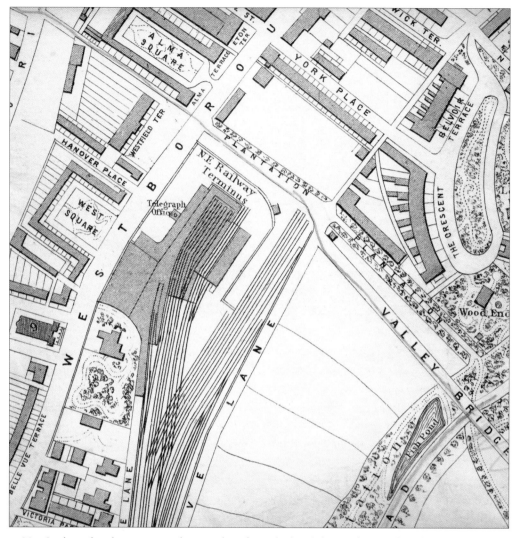

88 *Scarborough railway station and surroundings from Theakston's large-scale map of Scarborough published in the 1870s.*

The opening of the railway line to York, followed in 1846 by a branch from Seamer south down the coast to Filey, was a momentous event in the history of the town and heralded a period of unprecedented growth that saw Scarborough's population rise from just under 13,000 in 1851 to around thirty-three thousand by 1891. This growth in population meant there was a massive expansion in the size of the town. By the 1890s much of the land to the west that separated Scarborough from the nearby village of Falsgrave

had been swallowed up by buildings, mostly private houses, and southwards the development of the South Cliff took the edge of the built-up area to the foot of Oliver's Mount.

Initially the railway seems to have had a modest impact on the holiday trade of the town. The high cost of rail travel and the almost complete absence of leisure time among the working classes meant that, despite George Knowles's misgivings, the train brought mainly upper and middle-class visitors to Scarborough.

89 *The Crown Hotel was among the first buildings to be constructed on the South Cliff.*

This is reflected in the guidebooks of the 1850s and 1860s, which still focus largely on the refined attractions of the spa, the museum and rides in the countryside to the nearby picturesque villages of Hackness and Scalby, much as guides in the decades before the coming of the railway had recommended. Nevertheless, there was clearly a growth in the number of visitors coming to Scarborough by rail, resulting in the opening of several purpose-built hotels in competition with the well-established inns and lodging houses of the pre-railway era. The *Crown* on the Esplanade was the first, opening the year before the railway in 1844 as part of the early development of the South Cliff. Under its entrepreneurial first tenant, John Sharpin, who advertised the *Crown* in the London papers, the hotel quickly acquired the reputation of being the most elegant place to stay in the town. Sharpin began his working life apprenticed to a grocer in Ripon and, after a spell as a wine and spirit merchant in London, took over the tenancy of the *Crown Hotel* while still in his early twenties. He had a particular enthusiasm for advertising and once

at Scarborough set about raising awareness of the resort and the hotel as widely as he could, as 'In every newspaper and publication of the day were the beauties of Scarborough extolled in glorious but unexaggerated terms.' Sharpin was the first of a new breed of seaside entrepreneur who understood the importance of advertising and, coming from outside the town, could see the potential of Scarborough as a resort perhaps more clearly than those with local connections. Other large hotels opened soon after the *Crown*. The *Queen's Hotel* on the north side opened in 1848 with 100 bedrooms as part of a terrace overlooking the North Bay, while in the centre of the town the *Royal Hotel* in St Nicholas Street was extended around this time to incorporate Donner's former assembly rooms. Undoubtedly the most famous hotel to open in the decades immediately following the coming of the railway was the *Grand Hotel* on St Nicholas Cliff, financed by a group of Yorkshire businessmen and designed by the Leeds architect Cuthbert Brodrick. When it opened in 1867 it was reputed to be the largest hotel in Europe, with 365 bedrooms on 12 floors, and also the continent's largest brick building. The hotel occupies a commanding site overlooking the South Bay and the harbour and represents the most enduring monument to the early decades of Scarborough's railway era.

The railway itself soon became part of the entertainment on offer at Scarborough. With the opening of the branch line in 1847 to Pickering and Whitby at Rillington on the York to Scarborough line, visitors to Scarborough had the opportunity to explore the district more widely than before. Crosby's Scarborough guide, published around 1860, ends with a section entitled 'Railway Trips', describing day-ticket excursions to Castle Howard, Pickering and Whitby.

Scarborough as a Health Resort

In the 17th century it was the health-giving properties of the mineral spa that encouraged people to seek a cure at Scarborough. Bathing and swimming in the sea was a further enticement in the 18th century but it was arguably the growing belief in the health-giving properties of sea air in the middle of the 19th century that had the biggest impact on the town, as it encouraged many to take up permanent residence in Scarborough, as in other seaside towns. The curative properties and quality of the fresh air found at the seaside began to gain favour among the medical profession at the beginning of the 19th century and gained general acceptance in the 1850s. Scarborough doctors began extolling the benefits of year-round

90 *The* Queen's Hotel *opened in 1848 was the first large hotel on the north side.*

91 *The* Grand Hotel *has dominated the South Bay since it was opened in 1867.*

92 *The interior of the Grand Hotel, photographed around 1900.*

93 *A sandcastle-building competition in full swing around the turn of the 20th century.*

94 *Bathing machines were a common sight on the sands for around 200 years until the early 20th century.*

95 *The interior of a bathing machine as depicted in Crosby's Scarborough guide, published in the 1860s.*

residency at Scarborough for those seeking health, dispelling notions that the town was a bleak, damp place in the winter. Dr Breary, in his popular Medical Guide to Scarborough, published in several editions in the 1860s, claimed the atmosphere imparted buoyancy and made the elderly feel quite young again. Encouraged by these and similar claims many people moved to Scarborough, particularly after retirement, starting a trend that still continues to

this day and contributing to the rapid expansion of the built-up area of the town in the second half of the 19th century. Builders were warned that, unless they constructed better and more tenantable houses, Scarborough would never become an autumn and winter residence for the infirm and the retired and would fail to achieve its rightful status as 'the Brighton of the north'. Streets lined with villa residences spread between Scarborough and Falsgrave and on the South Cliff, where terraces of large private residences and apartments for visitors were laid out in the 1850s and 1860s behind and beyond the 1840s Esplanade. The development of the South Cliff was largely driven by private capital and controlled by the South Cliff Company, who were criticised in 1860 for allowing the development of the *Prince of Wales Hotel* forward of the line of the original Esplanade, thus interrupting the elegance of the terraced façade. The South Cliff rose in popularity as a residential area with the opening of the Valley Bridge in 1865, spanning the Ramsdale Valley to provide a level route for pedestrians and carriages from the railway station and the main shopping streets. The bridge was constructed by private capital under the auspices of the Valley Bridge Company, reusing the structure from the recently collapsed girder bridge across the River Ouse at Lendal in York. Tolls were set at half a pence for a pedestrian and three pence for any horse-drawn vehicle. The bridge was brought into public ownership in 1891 but a report in 1911 found that the structure had become too weak for the traffic of the day and was therefore substantially reconstructed with a wider carriageway in 1925. The bridge still carries the main route south from the town to Filey and Bridlington.

In 1858 the Corporation and representatives of the South Cliff Company formed a committee to raise funds to build a new church to serve

A fairly minor but still significant contribution to the growth of Scarborough's population after the 1850s was an expansion in the number of private educational establishments founded in the town. Scattered among the new villa residences of South Cliff and Falsgrave, the schools catered for the growing number of

96   *A fishing boat being unloaded on the beach in the 1850s.*

this rapidly expanding suburb. The company was gifted a plot of land in Albion Road but donations were slow to accumulate and building work did not start until a wealthy resident of the Esplanade, Miss Mary Craven, stepped in to guarantee the full amount of the construction costs. The church of St Martin-on-the-Hill was consecrated in April 1863 and is a fitting addition to this wealthy suburb, with interior decoration by the firm of Morris and Company including stained glass by the pre-Raphaelite artists Rossetti and Burne-Jones.

97   *A sketch by the artist Randolph Caldecott, published in 1878, showing visitors enjoying the sands.*

98   *Fun on the sands as sketched by Randolph Caldecott and published in 1878.*

99 *Engraving of the South Cliff from the 1870s, with St Martin's Church in the foreground and St Andrew's Church, opened in 1868, in the background.*

wealthy families choosing to set up home in the town as well as boarders from further afield. 'No more favoured locality for an educational centre, it is safe to assert, exists in the British Isles than Scarborough, which in the salubrity of it's site and the beauty of it's natural surroundings, presents unrivalled advantages for the purpose in view,' or so the advert for The Westland's High-class School for Girls in the Valley asserted towards the close of the century. Most boasted a broad curriculum, with languages, music and drawing offered alongside more academic subjects aimed at securing entry to Cambridge or Oxford universities or into the military and the Church. Sports and physical education were also important. Pupils at the Winterton School on the South Cliff had access to the courts of the North of England Lawn Tennis Club off Filey Road, while the Westlands School boasted a Swedish gymnasium and the attentions of a resident teacher engaged from the Hampstead Physical Training College.

Municipal Reform and Development

The passing of the Municipal Reform Act in December 1835 may be less celebrated in the history of the town than the coming of the railway but, without the reform of the Corporation that followed on from it, it is unlikely that Scarborough would have been able to make quite the massive strides forward that it did in the 1850s and 1860s. The Act swept away the old traditional systems of local government to replace them with a much more regularised and open system based on elections. Under the old system in Scarborough, local power rested with the 44 members of the town council who, though in theory were elected annually, were in actual fact drawn from a narrow circle of long-established Scarborough families to the virtual exclusion of new members. By the 1830s the council had acquired a reputation for corruption and excess, notoriously spending money earmarked for harbour repairs and other municipal improvements on celebrations and 'refreshments'. The tavern expenses for the council in 1833, for example, included £16 10s. on wine at the election of the junior bailiff in April and over £3 spent on wine and punch at the sale of Corporation lands held at the *Bell Inn* on Bland's Cliff. After the passing of the Act, the structure of Scarborough Corporation changed drastically, based on an electorate drawn from over 500 adult male ratepayers. The town was divided into north and south wards, each represented by nine councillors who were joined by six aldermen and a mayor. Although still far from representative of the entire town, the new structure broke the influence exerted by a minority of families and created the basis for a more forward-thinking local authority just at the time when Scarborough was facing the prospect of massive change with its connection to the railway network.

The reformed council soon started to bring much-needed improvements to the town for both residents and visitors alike. Chief of these was the improvement to the sewage system and the water supply, without which none of the expansion in the built-up area witnessed in the second half of the 19th century could have occurred on the scale that it did. While some in the Old Town had the benefit of private wells for their water, many of the poorest streets still relied on the medieval system of three conduits bringing water from the Falsgrave springs for their daily supply. From 1844 the council worked with the newly formed Scarborough Waterworks Company to secure a more copious supply of fresh water to the town by laying new pipes to connect to springs at the foot of the cliffs in Cayton Bay, about three miles to the south of the town, where a new steam-pumping station

was built to raise the water to a reservoir on the cliff top. This supply, augmented by a well nearer to Cayton village, provided 800,000-900,000 gallons of fresh water a day, sufficient to supply all the households in the growing town as well as flush out the tributary drains of the main sewers in the streets, alleys and small courts of the Old Town. A new main sewer was laid in 1848 to take the waste from the existing network of pipes out to sea beyond the West Pier. The refurbishment of the sewer pipes in St Sepulchre Street at this time unexpectedly brought to light the in-filled remains of a wide, deep ditch full of compressed decomposed vegetable matter resembling peat. The ditch was part of the town's defences constructed to protect the west side of the Old Borough in the middle of the 12th century and it had become so filled with rubbish in the Middle Ages that its precise location was lost until this discovery.

The sale of Corporation land on the South Cliff in the 1840s not only encouraged the early expansion of buildings in this area but also raised sufficient funds to build a new town gaol at the north end of St Thomas Street to replace the cramped cells contained within the main entrance into the town at Newborough Bar. Within 20 years this building also proved

100 *The cemetery depicted in 1863, six years after it opened.*

too cramped and comparatively easy to break out of, so the Corporation decided on a new prison on the northern outskirts of the town, in what is now Dean Road, in between a new workhouse to the south and the new cemetery to the north. The first workhouse was built by the Corporation in the 1740s, using income from the spa wells, on vacant land just to the north of Newborough Bar, where formerly had stood the medieval chapel of St Thomas. At the time of its removal to the new site in Dean Road, there were 92 inmates, including an 87-year-old flour miller from Malton, a 77-year-old farm labourer from Suffield and an unmarried mother from Norfolk with week-old twin boys. The new cemetery received its first burials in 1857.

The cemetery is still there, but the workhouse and gaol are long gone institutions. An enduring legacy of this period of municipal improvements is the market hall in the heart of the Old Town, opened in 1853. It replaced the outdoor butchers' quarter called The Shambles between St Helen's Square and Leading Post Street, which by the

1850s had become an annoyance to resident and visitor alike. A pamphlet published in 1850 by a 'lover of Scarborough and one interested in its prosperity' gives a vivid picture of The Shambles shortly before they were closed:

> Visitors are disgusted with the sight of animals slaughtered and dressed almost in our very streets, and at all hours of the day, and the carcasses with blood running from them, suspended over the footpath: the shambles appear as though they were not washed from one year's end to another.

The new market hall, designed by the Borough Surveyor John Irvine, remains in use as one of the Old Town's finest buildings.

The Late Victorian Resort

For most of the Victorian period the opportunity to spend a week or a fortnight at the seaside was restricted to the middle and upper classes. The most that working-class people could look forward to was a day trip on the train, made more possible in 1871 with the legislation introduced by Sir John Lubbock creating the first Bank

101   *The North Bay pier seen from the castle.*

102 *Victorian visitors enjoying the North Bay pier.*

Holiday. As a result, in the 1860s and 1870s, alongside the well-established attractions such as the spa and the museum, new attractions began to appear, aimed principally at the growing numbers of visitors with hours rather than days to spend in the town. The two most ambitious were the North Bay pleasure pier, opened in 1869, and the aquarium in the South Bay, completed in 1877.

After a number of abortive attempts to raise capital for a pleasure pier in the early 1860s, a consortium of local businessmen formed the Scarborough Promenade Pier Company in 1865 and appointed Eugenius Birch as engineer. Birch came with considerable experience of constructing pleasure piers at seaside resorts around the country and his design for Scarborough was for a 1,000ft-long promenade with an iron girder substructure built off cast-iron columns to be anchored on wooden piles driven into the foreshore. A saloon at the seawards end of the pier provided refreshments and a location

103 *The hall at the former Rock Gardens, depicted in the late 1860s at the foot of the cliff.*

for band concerts and religious services. With an entrance ticket costing just 1d the pier was initially popular with day trippers when it opened on 1 May 1869 but its comparative remoteness from Scarborough's other attractions and the nearly constant need for funds to repair storm damage meant that it was soon struggling to make a profit. The end for the pier came in January 1905 when the structure was badly damaged in a gale, leaving the saloon stranded out at sea. No serious consideration was given to rebuilding the pier and the remains were eventually sold for scrap.

Even before the construction of the pleasure pier, an attempt had been made to entice more visitors to the north side with the opening of the Rock Gardens on the cliff slope near the castle headland. The brainchild of a local engineer, Josiah Fairbank, the scheme turned 10 acres of the cliff side into a pleasure garden with terraced walks and a large entertainment hall capable of seating 3,000 people. Reached by what must have been a fairly daunting arch-covered wooden staircase from the cliff top, the gardens opened in July 1860 but only lasted for two years after suffering poor attendances and problems with cliff slumps.

The aquarium was by far the most ambitious attraction to open on the south side during the latter half of the 19th century, located in the valley immediately below the Cliff Bridge and therefore close to both the *Grand Hotel* and spa.

Both the hotel and the Corporation resisted the plans for such a populist venture in what was one of the more select parts of the town, but the opposition was eventually overcome and Eugenius Birch, architect of the North Bay pier, was appointed as engineer having previously designed the Brighton aquarium. Entirely underground, the three-acre interior housed a variety of exhibits and attractions that were meant both to instruct and entertain. Exotically decorated in a style described in one guidebook as 'Mohamedan-Indian', for an entrance ticket of 1s the visitor could see, housed in 25 tanks, alligators and seals and a wide variety of fish, as well as take advantage of a reading room and a dining room. Some 3,000-4,000 visitors entered on the opening day in May 1877 but the aquarium's popularity barely lasted a decade. By the 1880s the aquarium's strong educational and scientific tone no longer proved appealing and the business was sold at a loss to William Morgan, then manager of the Winter Gardens at Blackpool.

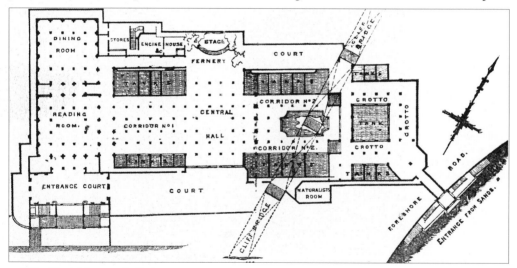

104 *Plan of the aquarium.*

105 *Artist's sketches of the interior of the aquarium from the May 1888 edition of the* Journal of Decorative Art.

In the firm belief that visitors 'would rather see a juggler than an uncooked lobster', Morgan relaunched the attraction as the Palace of Amusements, putting on a 10-hour programme of concerts, variety shows and swimming entertainments aimed primarily at the day visitor – 'the Greatest Sixpennyworth in the World' as Morgan's advert at the turn of the 20th century claimed.

Barely a stone's throw from the aquarium, the spa also had to adapt in the second half of the 19th century in response to the growing numbers of visitors. Historically the spa had been the preserve of the affluent and, although this did not change immediately with the coming of the railway to Scarborough, all the major changes that happened afterwards were in response to increasing numbers of visitors. When the railway opened in 1845 the spa was dominated by a large castellated saloon in the Gothic

106
The interior of the Victorian aquarium on Foreshore Road.

107 *The refreshment room at the aquarium, photographed at the turn of the 20th century.*

108 *The theatre at the aquarium, photographed at the end of the 19th century.*

109 *William Morgan took over the running of the People's Palace and aquarium in 1886.*

style designed by the London architect Henry Wyatt and opened in 1839. The saloon, along with a new sea wall and promenade incorporating the spa wells, was built by the Cliff Bridge Company after they took over the lease of the spa from the Corporation in 1827, replacing facilities that had not changed significantly since the middle of the 18th century. By the 1850s the saloon had outgrown its usefulness and in 1858 the Cliff Bridge Company replaced it with a new music hall to the design of Sir Joseph Paxton and enlarged the promenade to cope with increasing numbers of visitors. The music hall lasted barely 20 years before it was burnt down in 1877 to be replaced by an even larger grand hall designed by the London architects Verity and Hunt, incorporating a theatre, a large hall and rooms given over for receptions, reading, billiards and refreshments. With extensive gardens carved out of the cliff behind, the rebuilt spa may have offered a more refined atmosphere than the nearby aquarium but it had lost much of the exclusivity of earlier decades.

Access along the seafront to the aquarium and spa complex was made easier with the opening of Foreshore Road in 1877, which enabled people to approach from the direction of the harbour 'along a splendid promenade and carriage drive'. The opening of Foreshore Road was the first stage in the creation of a two-mile long promenade running between the North and South Bays around the foot of the headland, creating one of the finest seafronts in the country that has enduring appeal, and being the most impressive engineering feat in Scarborough since the construction of the castle keep in the 12th century. Marine Drive around the headland was the final and most difficult stage in the implementation of this plan, the work

110 *The old Newborough Bar was replaced in 1843 with a new entrance in the Gothic style. This was demolished in 1890 as a traffic hazard.*

111 *Wyatt's Gothic-style saloon of 1839 at the spa was replaced in 1858.*

112   *View of the grand hall at the spa shortly after its refurbishment following the fire of 1877.*

113   *Fashionable visitors enjoying the spa promenade at the end of the 19th century.*

114 *The sands before the opening of the Foreshore Road.*

115 *Victorians enjoying the newly completed Foreshore Road.*

116   *Sandside before the construction of Marine Drive.*

117   *Visitors enjoying the newly-opened Marine Drive.*

118 *Marine Drive opened in 1908, linking the North and South Bays.*

taking just over 10 years to complete between 1898 and 1908. In order to open up access to the South Bay end of Marine Drive, many old harbour-side buildings were demolished between 1902 and 1905 in order to create Sandside as a route linking back to Foreshore Road. This opened up the area closest to the harbour to the tourist trade, where formally the fishing and shipbuilding industries had dominated. Shipbuilding ended in 1863 with the closure of Tindall's yard, while the commercial centre

of the fishing industry moved to the West Pier. This pier started life in 1817 as a short timber and stone jetty opposite West Sandgate but was considerably extended, widened and heightened between 1877 and 1880 to create facilities for the landing, processing and selling of catches. The sight of 'Scottish fishing lassies', who followed arrived in Scarborough in the summer months to work on processing the catches, proved a popular sight with visitors in the decades either side of the start of the 20th century.

119 *The cover of this Edwardian guidebook conveys an impression of elegance.*

EIGHT

Scarborough in the 20th Century

Edwardian Scarborough

The years immediately before the outbreak of the First World War were a golden period for the resort, when Scarborough could justifiably claim to be 'The Queen of All Watering Places'. The town promoted its fashionable side to attract the upper and middle classes while the railway brought crowds of working-class day-trippers on organised excursions. No one social group dominated the resort, and even the spa, traditionally the most exclusive part of the town, still welcomed the day-tripper to enjoy its seafront promenade, orchestra recitals and gardens.

The excursion guide issued to employees of the brewery firm Bass, Ratcliff and Gretton of Burton upon Trent for their visit to Scarborough in 1914 (reprinted by the Bass Museum in 1977) gives a valuable insight into the workings of a day trip to Scarborough during the Edwardian period, which for most of the employees would have been their only seaside visit of the year. The firm organised the excursion with military precision, contacting various businesses and attractions in Scarborough well in advance to secure discounts for its employees. On the day of the excursion, Friday 24 July, 14 trains took the workforce on the four-hour journey to Scarborough, with staggered departure times from Burton Station beginning at the astonishingly early hour of 3.40 a.m. With only a five-minute break for refreshments at York, the excursionists alighted at Scarborough to find themselves not at the railway station but at the new excursion station half a mile to the west, which had opened in Londesborough Road in 1908 to handle the growing number of excursion trains coming to Scarborough during the season. With only 12 hours to spend in the resort, the first 15 minutes were perforce taken up walking into town or queuing up for a tram on Falsgrave Road to take them into the centre.

The opening of the tram network in 1904 was a major innovation of the Edwardian era, linking the main shopping streets and railway station with the North and South Bay seafronts. Even with the tram it would have been impossible to get around all the attractions on offer listed in the excursion guide. The harbour, the castle and the parish church are described for those with an interest in history while for those who just wanted to walk and relax in the sea air Scarborough had a wide choice of parks,

120 *The Clarence Gardens on the north cliff opened in 1887. The bandstand with its sheltering banks was later removed.*

gardens and promenades to choose from. Visiting gardens had long been a popular pastime in Scarborough. Bean's Gardens along the road out of the Newborough Gate, Pearson's Strawberry Tea Gardens at Falsgrave and 'The Grove' in the valley were private ventures that were popular in Regency times, while the Corporation created the first large public park called the Clarence Gardens overlooking the North Bay in 1887. A decade later and the borough engineer, Harry Smith, began an ambitious programme of creating new public gardens at various locations around the town, most notably on the north side with the opening of the Alexandra Gardens on the north cliff in 1907 and Peasholm Park and lake in 1911-12. In 1914 the then newly opened park was described as 'laid out on Japanese lines, with a quaint rainbow bridge connecting the island with the mainland, an ornamental Boathouse, waterfalls, cascades and miniature lakes beyond'.

In view of the limited time available, most day excursionists probably never left the South Bay seafront. By 1914 the number and variety of attractions capable of accommodating large numbers, especially in wet weather, had grown from the original People's Palace and aquarium of 1877. Along Foreshore Road there was now Catlin's Arcadia, opened in 1909, which could accommodate an audience of 3,000 to watch the pierrot shows, and no fewer than three picture houses; the Palladium Picture House, the Olympia Picture Palace and the Grand Picture House. Sea and boat trips were on offer at the harbour while the bathing vans run by Mr Rawlings were available to the day-trippers at 4d per person to take a swim in the sea. The excursionists of 1914 would have been among the last to use the bathing machines on the south sands, as the opening of the South Bay swimming pool in 1915 to the south of the spa left no demand for them.

To appeal to those with money who could afford to stay at Scarborough, the council's Advertising Committee chose to emphasise the more romantic aspects of the town:

> The lover of life and fashion rejoices in the Spa and Esplanade. The poetically minded will turn to its romantic surroundings. The artist and the seekers after the quaint and picturesque will climb the awkward little streets and stairways of 'Old Scarborough,' which nestles under the castle Hill, studying sea-faring life down by the Harbour. The invalid will derive benefit from a climate which a dozen high authorities have praised for its dryness and equable temperature. The geologist, the archaeologist, and the naturalist each find something which no other place can offer.

The number and variety of hotels and boarding houses had grown rapidly during the last decades of the 19th century and by 1910 the town had around twenty large hotels, 50 smaller 'private' hotels and guest houses and well over a hundred furnished apartments to let, with accommodation to suit most pockets. Whereas a week at one of the large hotels such as the *Grand* or the *Pavilion* could cost between 3 and 4 guineas a week, the smaller hotels and boarding houses advertised daily rates of just a few shillings to appeal to those on tighter budgets taking shorter stays. The spa, with its grand hall, theatre, picture gallery, café, billiard room and spacious promenade, remained the centre of social life for the fashionable visitor. It was where 'everybody who is anybody lounges at some period of the day listening to a high-class band… and watching either the passing procession of beautiful ladies and beautiful dresses, or the ever varying sea pictures in the distance'. Drinking the mineral waters had fallen from favour and is hardly ever mentioned in promotional literature of the period. The highlight of the social week was to participate in the 'church parade' after morning service on a Sunday. Thousands turned out in their best attire to walk between the *Crown*

121 *The floral hall in the Alexandra Gardens was opened in 1912 and staged the Fols-de-Rols theatrical entertainment. It was demolished in 1989.*

and *Prince of Wales Hotel* on the South Cliff or along Queen's Parade on the north side. The parade was said to be unmatched as a spectacle by any other resort in the country and was a favourite subject for the photographers of the period. It continued the tradition of promenading at Scarborough first recorded a century before on The Cliff.

Away from the spa, Edwardian Scarborough boasted a range and quality of shops not seen in earlier generations and largely supported, one suspects, by the purses of its more well-off visitors. Westborough, Newborough and St Nicholas Street contained the more fashionable shops and chief among these was the department store run by the firm of W. Rowntree and Sons in Westborough. Founded in the 1780s as a drapery business, by 1900 it had expanded to include clothing, furnishing and the decorative arts, specialising in pieces in the Oriental style. The business occupied an imposing purpose-built store of four storeys constructed in 1882 in the French Renaissance style and boasted an hydraulic lift running between the floors. Those who remember it still lament its closure and demolition in 1987. Lower down Westborough, the showroom of J. Tonks and Sons sold high-quality furniture, carpets, tapestries and linoleums and had enjoyed the patronage of King Edward VII when still Prince of Wales. Away from the more fashionable streets, 'The

122 *The pierrot show was the main attraction at Catlin's Arcadia on the foreshore.*

123 *The Pavilion Hotel opened in 1870 on a prominent corner site opposite the railway station.*

Remnant Warehouse' in Market Street, run by William Boyes, sold all kinds of clothing, bric-a-brac and fancy goods at bargain prices, packed into an interior that was likened to an oriental bazaar. The warehouse attracted far more locals than the more affluent shops in the upper part of the town and as Boyes' Store it continues in business to this day.

Outwardly, the Edwardian period brought many improvements to the town with the laying out of new parks and gardens, the introduction of the tram network and the opening of Marine Drive. But the changes masked underlying problems with poverty and unemployment. Scarborough was by now first and foremost a holiday resort, with all the employment problems

124   *The wine cellar of the* Pavilion Hotel. *The contents were auctioned off in 1970 and the hotel was demolished in 1973.*

125   *The* Victoria Hotel *was run by the Laughton family at the end of the 19th century, who went on to own both the* Pavilion *and* Royal *hotels.*

126 *Sunday church parade on the Esplanade.*

THE ESPLANADE FROM PRINCE OF WALES HOTEL.

128 *Newborough at the end of the 19th century.*

127 *The church parade on the Esplanade as depicted by John Dinsdale in 1880.*

129 *The exterior of Rowntree's store. The building was demolished to make way for the Brunswick Shopping Centre, which opened in 1991.*

130 *Rugs and carpets on display in Rowntree's department store at the start of the 20th century.*

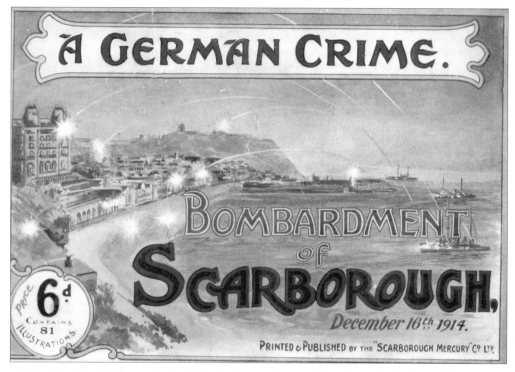

131 *Several booklets appeared after the bombardment and were used as propaganda for the war effort.*

this brought in the winter months when many shops and attractions closed down, including much of the tram network. An allied problem was the poor living conditions in the Old Town, with many residents forced to live in cramped, squalid conditions that the next generation would condemn as slums. However the outbreak of war in August 1914 delayed significant change for a decade.

Bombardment

The First World War was barely four months old when the conflict was brought suddenly to Scarborough with the German naval bombardment of Wednesday 16 December 1914. Starting at around 8 a.m., the German battleships Derflinger and Von Der Tonn shelled the castle and town for half an hour in a bombardment that has gone down in history as the first attack on a civilian population in modern warfare. Damage to property was widespread. Eighteen

men, women and children lost their lives and many others were injured.

The battleships had spent some time immediately before dawn on 16 December at anchor several miles to the north, but as night started to lift they set off down the

132 *Artist's reconstruction of German shells hitting the castle. The castle was the first part of the town to be targeted.*

133 *The curtain wall of the castle was breached by German shells.*

134 *The barracks in the castle grounds was not rebuilt after the bombardment.*

135 *Many shops and houses were damaged in the bombardment. This is Joseph Merryweather's grocery shop at 43 Prospect Road.*

coast, arriving half a mile off shore at around 8 a.m. The battleships were first spotted by the Admiralty coastguard stationed on the castle headland, who managed to send a warning and seek shelter before the first shells arrived. The coastguard station was flattened, along with the long-deserted 18th-century barracks on the curtain wall, which was reduced to rubble after being hit by six shells. After several minutes the battleships turned their fire away from the castle and onto the town and, for the next half-hour, 500 shells rained down on the inhabitants. A postman was killed on his rounds, a 15-year-old boy died on his way to buy a paper and, in the worst single incident, a mother and three of her children lost their lives when no. 2 Wykeham Street received a direct hit. Roofs were blown off and windows shattered in street after street until, after about fifteen minutes, firing ceased to allow the battleships to turn and head back northwards. With the manoeuvre completed, the firing recommenced and continued for about another fifteen minutes until, with one parting shot, the Germans hit the middle of the lighthouse, which had to be demolished several days later. At 9 a.m. the vessels appeared off Whitby, where they shelled the town and abbey for 11 minutes before turning eastwards away from the coast.

Not unexpectedly, many people feared the bombardment was the precursor to a German invasion. Huge crowds flocked to the railway station in an effort to escape the town while others took to the roads to head inland in search of safety. Troops stationed at barracks a mile north of the town took up defensive positions along the cliff tops, while reinforcements were brought in by train from York. The invasion never came as the bombardment of Scarborough and Whitby and an attack on Hartlepool the same day by another part of the enemy fleet were part of a concerted plan on the part of

136 *Design for a poster taking the 1914 bombardment of Scarborough as its theme.*

the German navy to expose the vulnerability of the English coast to attack and provide a diversion while other ships laid a minefield. The British government was quick to exploit the bombardment for propaganda as the town had no military significance, which made the attack appear all the more barbaric. This was not to be the end of Scarborough's direct experience

137   *Scarborough was visited by the British fleet soon after the end of the First World War.*

138   *The South Bay swimming pool opened in 1915 and was initially very popular with bathers and spectators alike. It closed in 1989 and has since been filled in.*

of war. Many Scarborough fishing vessels were sunk with the loss of crewmen and the town was struck again from the sea on the evening of 4 September 1917, when a German U-boat surfaced to fire 30 shells at minesweepers in the bay and at the town itself, killing three people and seriously injuring five others. By the armistice in November 1918, 747 men, women and children from Scarborough had lost their lives in the war, to whose lasting memory the town unveiled the war memorial on Oliver's Mount on 26 September 1923.

Between the Wars

In the three years immediately after the end of the First World War it was reported that visitors returned in large numbers to Scarborough during the summer months and, in 1921, an entertainments manager was appointed by the council to organise events in Peasholm Park and at the South Bay bathing pool to revitalise these relatively new attractions, and also the castle, which the council had taken on lease from the Government Office of Woods and Forests in 1906. Prior to that date the war department used the headland for military training, including rifle and artillery practice, and continued to use the site sporadically after it was leased to the council. In 1907 the council set about restoring the keep and landscaping the grounds to make the site more welcoming to visitors and they agreed to let the organising committee of the Scarborough Historical Pageant and Play stage the performances in the castle grounds in July and August 1912. The pageant involved hundreds of local people in period costumes re-enacting historical episodes from Scarborough's history in front of a paying audience of up to three thousand. The event took 18 months to plan and included designing and erecting a curving wooden stand on the headland facing towards the keep to accommodate the audience. The performances were meant to educate as well as

entertain and were the first time that the history of the town had been popularised and brought before a mass audience.

The idea of open-air performances first attempted on a large scale on the castle headland seems to have lodged with some in the council because in the 1930s the development of an open-air theatre on the north side formed a major part of the efforts to develop the North Bay for visitors. Building on the success of the pre-war Peasholm Park, the foresighted borough engineer Harry Smith continued to enhance the physical layout of the Peasholm area in 1924 with the extension of the Glen gardens along the valley that fed Peasholm Lake. The following year the council opened the Corner Café, with large windows looking across the bay towards the castle, on the North Bay seafront, followed in 1928 by the creation by Smith of the North Bay Pleasure Gardens on the adjacent 27 acres of land. This was arguably Smith's most ambitious garden creation as it included the construction of an artificial lake in the valley that cut down to the sea beyond the Corner Café, alongside which was laid the track of a miniature railway that ran through the gardens for over a mile to a terminus at the furthest part of the North Bay at Scalby Mills. The railway opened in 1931, followed the next year by the Open Air Theatre, which took advantage of the natural acoustics of the valley. A stage was created on an island in the lake with room for lavish backdrops overlooked by seating for up to 5,000 rising in tiered rows up the valley side. Staging musicals and light operas, the theatre was hugely popular with visitors in the 1930s, who were urged not to miss 'the truly breathtaking, floodlit spectacle of the Open-Air Theatre', so much so that an extra 2,000 seats had to be added soon after it opened.

The council's development of the north side preserved the distinct character of the area from

139 *The Scarborough pageant of July 1912 took 18 months to plan but made a financial loss. It was staged again in August in an effort to increase profits.*

140 *A group of Edward I's knights from the 1912 pageant photographed at the keep.*

141 *Advert for Rowntree's store at the time of the Scarborough pageant.*

142 *The castle grounds in the 1930s with a scattering of tents.*

143 *Clearance of slum properties in the Old Town brought to light traces of medieval buildings including this massive stone wall, possibly part of the Dominican friary.*

the kind of commercial tourist development that characterised the South Bay. To Scarborough's advantage, this distinction still largely persists to this day, giving the North Bay more of a quieter, family appeal at times when the South Bay is at its most crowded. A large part of this is down to the vision of Harry Smith, whose energy and talents were also directed at regenerating parts of the Old Town in the 1920s and 1930s, replacing blocks of derelict houses and slum dwellings with new flats and houses. By 1936, 412 slum dwellings had been demolished and a total area of 5.5 acres rebuilt in the historic centre of Scarborough, satisfying a pressing need to improve the living conditions of some of the poorest members of Scarborough's population. An unexpected consequence of this rebuilding work was that it brought parts of the medieval town to light,

including 'peat deposits' and wells in the Cross Street and Friargate areas and a series of massive stone walls that may have been part of the medieval Dominican friary situated between Queen Street and Cross Street.

Alongside the rebuilding of parts of the Old Town between 1925 and 1929, the new housing estates of Northstead, Stepney, Newlands, Barrowcliff and Prospect Mount extended the urban area westwards and northwards toward the hamlets of Throxenby and Newby. To the south, large-scale development was impossible because of the high ground of Seamer Moor and Oliver's Mount. The Edgehill Estate was built in this direction along the main road heading south along the Seamer Valley, but large-scale development had to wait until 1950 with the construction of the Eastfield Estate situated below the southern flank of Oliver's Mount.

144 *Architect's drawing of one of the new houses offered for sale in the Stepney Close development on the western edge of the town, one of the suburbs that grew up in the 1920s and 1930s.*

145 *Adshead's proposed scheme for a development at Scalby Mills. A version of this scheme was constructed in the 1960s.*

146 *The steady development of the Peasholm area in the 1930s drew larger numbers of visitors to the North Bay.*

At the outbreak of the Second World War in 1939 Scarborough was preparing to embark on a new phase of urban improvements. Harry Smith retired from his post as Borough Engineer in 1933 after 35 years' service, so the council turned to the Emeritus Professor of Town Planning at London University, Stanley Adshead, to provide the vision for the further development of Scarborough. His authoritative and wide-ranging report included plans for 'improving existing places of Amusement and Recreation, and for the provision of new ones', local improvements to the seafront and the central part of the town and ideas to improve the approach routes to Scarborough. He specifically recommended the demolition of the Victorian aquarium on Foreshore Road, the building of a new entertainment complex in the North Bay

at Scalby Mills, to include a new outdoor pool (both of which had to wait until the 1960s), and the construction of a second outdoor pool at Peasholm next to the Corner Café. This scheme was put into immediate effect by adapting an existing children's boating pond.

The Second World War

By the outbreak of the Second World War Scarborough had enjoyed two decades of steady improvement in the living conditions of its inhabitants and in the quality of the holiday experience it could offer to its summer visitors. The range of parks, gardens and promenades, the new sporting facilities such as the North Bay Pool and the availability of unspoilt countryside close at hand to appeal to the new pursuit of 'rambling' led the council in the late 1930s to

147 *The North Bay Pool is in the foreground of this image from a 1950s guidebook.*

rebrand Scarborough as 'The Tonic Holiday', an interesting new take on the old theme of Scarborough as a health resort.

The first major impact of the Second World War on the town was the arrival in September 1939 of thousands of evacuees from Hull, Middlesbrough and other towns and cities under potential threat of aerial bombardment. However, Scarborough was not to escape the war unscathed by air attack. The first bombs were dropped on the town in June 1940. In October a parachute mine exploded below the castle dykes, laying waste the Potter Lane area, and the following March Scarborough was subjected to its own 'blitz' when around ninety enemy aircraft bombarded the town for several hours, destroying or damaging 1,378 buildings and killing 27 people. During the early years

of the war it was impossible for Scarborough to function as a holiday resort. Access to the beach was impossible, with large parts enclosed by barbed wire and laid with mines against a seaborne attack. Many hotels and boarding houses were requisitioned by the military to house service personnel, while the castle housed an RAF direction-finding station. Through use of high-frequency radio broadcasts from a polygonal wooden tower on the edge of the cliff the station helped Allied aircraft to navigate. It is also thought that the castle housed a top-secret listening station connected with the now famous code-breaking and intelligence establishment at Bletchley Park in Buckinghamshire. During this period Scarborough was protected by a coastal defence battery positioned on the cliff top at Wheatcroft, about two miles to the south of the castle. The battery possessed two six-inch calibre guns housed in protective shelters which, along with the battery searchlights, gave protection to the bay, day or night. There is no record of the guns ever being fired in anger or of the battery coming under attack from the air or the sea.

Some semblance of normal life for the resort returned in April 1942 with the reopening of a portion of the South Bay beach daily between 6 and 10 a.m and 5 and 9 p.m.. The north side and foreshore remained off limits.

The Modern Town

It was not until the start of the 1950s that life in Scarborough returned to something like pre-war normality. Though food rationing was still in force, the various hotels and boarding houses requisitioned by the military were returned to civilian use in 1947 and the summer crowds started to return. However, the town failed to invest in any major new attractions during the 1950s and 1960s. The most ambitious scheme of the 1950s was the Tree Walk, which opened in Peasholm Park in 1953. Designed around a meandering path through the treetops of Peasholm Park, 'children of all ages' were treated to models of 'charmingly quaint animals and insects, giant toadstools, the Mad Hatter, leaping frogs and timid rabbits, all illuminated from within'. The 1960s brought the development of an entertainment complex including a public house, amusement arcade and outdoor swimming pool at Scalby Mills in the North Bay, broadly in keeping with the proposals put forward in Stanley Adshead's report of 1938. Opened in 1966, the *New Scalby Mills Hotel* development struggled to attract large numbers and was demolished in 1988, joining the list of attractions stretching back into the 19th century that had failed on the north side. As the 1960s wore on Scarborough began to look rather staid and

traditional in the face of the growing competition from cheap package holidays to the continent and the 'holiday camp' experience offered by firms such as Butlins and Pontin's. The demolition of the *Pavilion Hotel* opposite the railway station in 1973, one of Scarborough's grandest and most prominent Victorian hotels, symbolised the resort's continuing decline in the 1970s, since when many small and medium-sized hotels have been converted into private apartments or self-catering accommodation.

Part of the problem facing Scarborough was the burden of having to maintain a diverse range of attractions inherited from the past. The upkeep of the vast acreage of public parks and gardens created in the late 19th and early 20th centuries were a drain on finances, while in 1966

148   *The spa lit up for an evening's entertainment in the late 1930s.*

the council finally lost the battle to keep Galaland open. This vast underground entertainment complex at the end of Foreshore Road that had begun as the People's Palace and aquarium in 1877 was demolished in 1968 and the site converted to an underground car park. The spa came back into the Corporation's hands in 1957 but it took over 20 years to agree plans on how to restore the historic Victorian buildings at the heart of the complex. Eventually, in 1981, the 1870s grand hall was re-opened after a lengthy period of restoration and continues to host shows and major conferences. The same year the spa waters were declared unfit for human consumption, so bringing to an end the use of the medicinal spring that played such an important part in shaping the town's development in the 17th and 18th centuries.

During the last 20 years several major projects have come to fruition, giving the town a more diverse appeal. The opening of the Sea Life Centre in the North Bay in 1991, the Stephen Joseph Theatre in the former Odeon cinema opposite the railway station in 1996 and the William Smith Museum of Geology in 2008 have brought Scarborough to the attention of new audiences in search of education and culture.

A recurring difficulty for Scarborough throughout its history has been that of inland communications. In the early period of the spa in the 17th and 18th centuries the easiest way to get to Scarborough was to come by sea, so bad were the roads inland. A canal was proposed in the 18th century to get around the problem of moving goods to and from the port, but this came to nothing and things only improved after the arrival of the railway in 1845. However, since the 1960s people have deserted public transport in favour of private vehicles. The A64 from York is the busiest route to Scarborough and is now blighted by slow-moving traffic at times in the summer months. Though the opening of the

149 *The Scarborough and District Archaeological Society (now the Scarborough Archaeological and Historical Society) was founded in 1947 and has done a great deal to research the archaeology of the town and the surrounding district. Here, members are shown excavating at Ayton Castle in 1958.*

Malton by-pass in 1979 alleviated the traffic jams in Malton town centre, the failure to make the A64 into a dual carriageway for the entire 40-mile journey from York is felt by many to be limiting Scarborough's future prosperity. Poor communications not only deter summer visitors but are a handicap to the development of the town as a centre for light industry and business, much of which is focussed on purpose-built industrial estates to the south of the town at Eastfield. One of the first firms to set up in this

150   *The Stephen Joseph Theatre opened in the former Odeon cinema building in 1996.*

part of the town was the coach-building firm of Plaxton, which opened its first factory on Seamer Road in 1936 and the site at Eastfield in 1961. The 1990s saw the expansion of Scarborough Business Park across an area of former gravel pits between Eastfield and Crossgates and now, with a supermarket and various car showrooms, the area is one of the busiest parts of the town.

The discussion document 'A Vision for Scarborough's Future', commissioned jointly by Scarborough Borough Council and Yorkshire Forward in 2002, reaffirmed the need for the town to diversify and 'recreate itself as a multi-faceted masterpiece', drawing on its heritage and culture for inspiration. The opening in 2008 of the Creative Industries Centre at Woodend delivered on the vision. With 52 office units and artists studios the centre aims to help develop new businesses and jobs and support cultural regeneration. This spirit of enterprise, together with other projects taking place in the town, led to Scarborough receiving the accolade of most enterprising place in Europe in the 2009 European Enterprise Awards. Scarborough appears to be on the verge of opening a new chapter in its long and eventful history.

BIBLIOGRAPHY

Adshead, Stanley, *Scarborough: A Survey of its Existing Conditions and some Proposals for its Future Development* (1938)

Baker, Joseph, *The History of Scarbrough* (1882)

Bayliss, Anne and Paul, *Architects and Civil Engineers of 19th Century Scarborough: A Biographical Dictionary* (2001)

Bayliss, Anne and Paul, *Scarborough's MPs 1832-1906: Scarborough's Mayors 1836-1906: A Biographical Dictionary* (2008)

Berryman, Bryan, *Scarborough as it Was* (1974)

Binns, Jack, *A Place of Great Importance: Scarborough in the Civil Wars 1640-1660* (1996)

Binns, Jack, *The History of Scarborough* (2001)

Crouch, David and Pearson, Trevor (eds), *Medieval Scarborough: Studies in Trade and Civic Life* (2001)

Edwards, Mervyn (ed.), *Scarborough 966-1966* (1966)

Hinderwell, Thomas, *The History and Antiquities of Scarborough* (1798)

Jeayes, Isaac, *Description of Documents contained in The White Vellum Book of the Scarborough Corporation* (1914)

Jones, James, *The German Attack on Scarborough* (1989)

Lidster, Robin, *Scarborough Railway Station: From Steam Age to Diesel Era* (1995)

Marsden, Barry, *Scarborough Tramways* (2007)

Pearson, Trevor, *The Archaeology of Medieval Scarborough* (2005)

Percy, Richard, *Scarborough: A Pictorial History* (1995)

Robertson, Alan, *Scarborough: The First Thousand Years* (1966)

Rowntree, Arthur (ed.), *The History of Scarborough* (1931)

Scarborough and District Civic Society, *The Streets of Scarborough* (2007)

Scarborough Archaeological and Historical Society, *A Guide to Historic Scarborough* (2003)

Transactions of the Scarborough Archaeological and Historical Society

Whittaker, Meredith, *The Book of Scarbrough Spaw* (1984)

INDEX

Note: Numbers in **bold** refer to illustrations

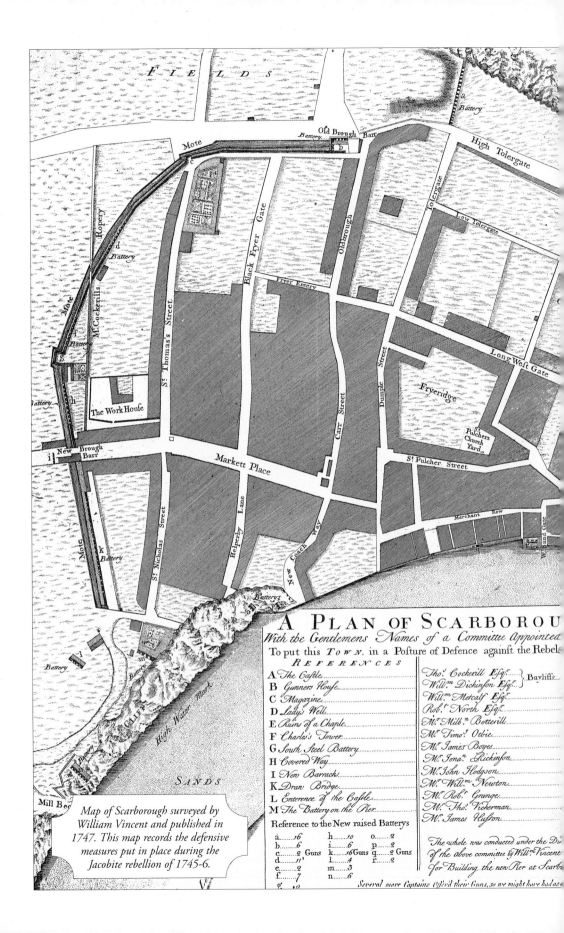

Map of Scarborough surveyed by William Vincent and published in 1747. This map records the defensive measures put in place during the Jacobite rebellion of 1745-6.